THE RELIGIOUS LIFE OF INDIA

THE SADHS

THE RELIGIOUS LIFE OF INDIA

THE SADHS

BY

W. L. ALLISON, B.A., B.D.

AMERICAN PRESBYTERIAN MISSION, GWALIOR

PILGRIMS

PILGRIMS PUBLISHING

◆ Varanasi ◆

THE SADHS The Religious Life Of India
W. L. ALLISON

Published by:
PILGRIMS PUBLISHING

An imprint of:
PILGRIMS BOOK HOUSE
(Distributors in India)
B 27/98 A-8, Nawabganj Road
Durga Kund, Varanasi-221010, India
Tel: 91-542- 2314060, 2312456
E-mail: pilgrims@satyam.net.in
Website: www.pilgrimsbooks.com

PILGRIMS BOOK HOUSE (New Delhi)
9 Netaji Subhash Marg, 2nd Floor
Near Neeru Hotel, Daryaganj, New Delhi 110002
Tel: 91-11-23285081 Fax: 91-11-23285722
E-mail: pilgrim@del2.vsnl.net.in

Distributed in Nepal by:
PILGRIMS BOOK HOUSE
P O Box 3872, Thamel, Kathmandu, Nepal
Tel: 977-1-4700942, Off: 977-1-4700919
Fax: 977-1-4700943
E-mail: pilgrims@wlink.com.np

Cover design by Asha Mishra

ISBN: 81-7769-345-X

Printed in India at Pilgrim Press Pvt. Ltd. Lalpur Varanasi

PREFACE TO THE NEW EDITION

The Sadhs are a very interesting group found mainly in North India. Concentrations of these faithful believers are found in Delhi, Farrukhabad and further east around Mirzapur. Other groups are found around Jaipur, Agra, Dolopur, Bharatpur, Jodhpur, and Rohtak. They are found in urban centres and as *jats*, rural farmers in the Punjab and Harayana. Traditionally, weaving seems to have been one of their main sources of income.

It is fairly certain that the Sadhs owe their origins to a figure known as Birbhal. The date given for this beginning is 1544. Another key figure in the development of the Sadhs, as a religious sect was Jogi Das. He was not a disciple, but effectively enlarged the precepts of the beliefs, possibly by incorporating some elements from Christianity. He dates from around 1658.

The religious buildings of the Sadhs are devoid of furniture, idols, rugs, furniture, decoration or anything, which might appeal to the emotions.

But what else do we know of the Sadh traditions? The Nirvana Ghan is their holy scripture, but copies of it are rare and fiercely guarded. The Bani Hymns of the Sadhs are an earlier source of their literature. A few lines from the text below give us an illumination of some of their main codes of practice.

"The Sadhs profess to abstain from all the luxuries; such as tobacco, betel, opium and wine. They never have exhibitions of dancing. All violence to man and beast is forbidden, but in self-defence, resistance is allowable. The Sadhs, like the Quakers, take great care of their poor and infirm people...All parade of

worship is forbidden. The due regulation of the tongue is a principle duty."

The Sadhs are neither Hindu nor Christian, but encompass elements from both ideas. They do have some elements of caste, though, and their prime development took place long after Christian ideas had spread from the Middle East to India. They are a stricter group, more orthodox and conservative, much like the puritan Amish of Pennsylvania in America perhaps?

This book, collated and written by W. L. Allison, brings all the sources and strands of information together, giving us a fascinating overview of this unusual and little-known group called the Sadhs.

Bob Gibbons

Siân Pritchard-Jones

Kathmandu 2004

PREFACE

THE opportunity for this study arose from the fact that in the spring of 1920 the writer was elected to the Bernardine Orme Smith Fellowship of the Presbyterian Theological Seminary of Chicago (then called the McCormick Theological Seminary). By special arrangement the rule of resident study was waived, and the writer was able at once to accept his missionary appointment to India.

The writer's interest in the Sadhs was aroused by conversations with Dr. Robert E. Speer and with the late Sir James Ewing. He remembers with gratitude the invaluable aid given him by Dr. H. D. Griswold, formerly of Lahore, and also by the late Professor J. N. Farquhar. A word of appreciation is also due to the Librarian of Farrukhabad, to the Librarian of Bhopal State, and to several Sadhs and others who helped to make possible the completion of this monograph.

The 1920 Smith Fellow never had the pleasure of meeting Colonel Smith the founder of the Fellowship Fund. Mrs. Smith approved of this unusual use of the Fellowship funds and, as long as she lived, manifested a genuine interest in the research.

It is a privilege to have this treatise published in the 'Religious Life of India' series.

For the sake of simplicity diacritical marks have been omitted.

Gwalior, India,
September, 1935.

TABLE OF CONTENTS

PART I

PART II

PART I

CHAPTER I

THE SADHS IN GENERAL

THE Sadhs are a group of people all belonging to one religious sect. Their history runs back about four hundred years. Outwardly they are Hindus, but many of their religious tenets vary greatly from orthodox Hinduism. They are chiefly drawn from the middle class; and some of them might be classed as wealthy. They form a non-idolatrous, monotheistic group, whose beliefs are composed of various elements gathered from several other religions and cults. Scholars, missionaries, and travellers have been interested in the Sadhs almost from the beginning of the modern missionary movement. Some people have compared them with the Friends; others, with the Jews. In 1924, the late Dr. J. N. Farquhar, in a letter to the writer, said:

> The facts, as you state them, prove the Sadhs to be one of the most interesting of the many religious groups found in North India. I did not realize that there is so much in their system to attract both the scholar and the religious man.

LOCATION

The Sadhs are found chiefly in the central part of India. The largest group is in Farrukhabad, United Provinces, a city situated about eighty miles up the Ganges River from Cawnpore. The second largest group is also in the United Provinces, in Mirzapur, south-east of Benares. These two groups represent the two most important urban communities. Village Sadhs are found in Bareilly, Shahjahanpur and Meerut, in the United Provinces. Groups, large and small, are to be round scattered all over the Delhi Province, and in Rohtak District in the Punjab, just north of Delhi; and also in the native states of Jind, Jaipur, Jodhpur, Dholpur and Bharatpur. The fact that some are city dwellers and others are rural folks partly explains the rather widespread area of their settlements.

Number

No one knows just how many Sadhs there are. Their influence extends far beyond what their paucity of numbers would lead us to expect. About 2,000 live in Farrukhabad; and nearly 1,000 in Mirzapur. Of the village groups, the largest known to the writer has a Sadh population of about 500. The smaller village groups will aggregate altogether about 2,500, which number, added to the above figures, gives as a result a possible maximum of 6,000 Sadhs. The fact that many Sadhs are enumerated in census reports as Hindus makes the task of calculation very difficult.

Throughout nearly the whole of their history, the Sadhs have attracted the attention of officials and historians. The excellence of their religious tenets, together with their industry and exemplary lives, has tended to make the Sadhs an outstanding community. During the past two generations the Farrukhabad Sadhs have become known not only in India, but also in the West, because of their industry of cloth-printing. Both the city and the rural Sadhs have at times been the objects of missionary effort. Dayananda, the founder of the Arya Samaj, made a careful study of the special points of Sadh doctrine.

Previous Articles on the Sadhs

Prior to this present attempt, no less than half a dozen writers have published articles explaining the religion and the customs of the Sadhs. The longest treatise was from the pen of the Rev. Henry Fisher, who as long ago as 1819 published in missionary annals a rather comprehensive account of the rural Sadhs, living just north of Delhi. This article is reprinted in Chapter III. In 1827, an Englishman, Mr. William Trant, prepared a short paper on the Farrukhabad Sadhs, and this document will be found in Chapter IV. Then in 1822 Mr. H. H. Wilson, of the Indian Medical Service, published a monograph dealing with all communities of the Sadhs. Next, in 1896, Sir William Crooke, of the Indian Civil Service, included an interesting and largely original paper on the Sadhs in his *Tribes and Castes of the North-West Provinces.*[1] Much of Sir W. Crooke's material will be found in Chapters VIII and IX of the present work. Dr. G. A. Grierson prepared a summary of these articles for the ninth volume of Hastings' *Encyclopædia of Religion and Ethics.* One other name remains to be mentioned, who, although his writings have never been published, was perhaps the most thorough of all those who have studied the Sadhs—the late Dr. J. N. Farquhar, already quoted. His interpretation of the early history of the Sadhs appears in Chapter V. In addition to these articles in English, two or three local men of Farrukhabad (one of them a non-Sadh) have written articles in Hindi on the Sadhs. It is because of the incomplete English documents, most of which are now inaccessible to the public, that Dr. H. D. Griswold of Lahore expressed his opinion several years ago that there was a real need for an up-to-date monograph on the Sadhs.

Early History Not Recorded

The early history of the Sadhs still lies in obscurity. They have never received any more than casual attention from the writers of secular history, largely because their numbers have not justified an exhaustive study. The fact that the sect had its origin in a period of much turbulence and confusion, makes it now well-nigh impossible to disentangle the record of this small community from the history of several contemporaneous sects. Added to this is the fact that Sadhs themselves have not had the interest and training to enable them to prepare and trace any exact account of their own development.

In general, two conclusions may be drawn from this brief survey. First, the Sadh religion undoubtedly had its beginning in a religious awakening. The 'charter members' of the Sadh sect had the zeal of new religious converts, as well as strength to withstand ridicule and persecution. Secondly, it was not only a movement towards a new and purer religion, but it was a reform movement, that is, a revolt. The first Sadh converts had discovered something better than the religion of their fathers, and they knew it beyond the peradventure of a doubt. In other words, they were 'Protestants' moving towards a Puritanism. The brief account in the *Farrukhabad* (*U.P.*) *Gazetteer* runs as follows:

> The Sadhs are a caste which is almost peculiar to Farrukhabad, though there are one or two small colonies elsewhere. They were returned at the census[1] as a Hindu caste, and it has been judicially held that the Hindu law of succession applies to them, but they would perhaps prefer rather to be regarded as an independent sect, for they follow none of the ordinary practices of Hinduism.[2]

In the first century of their history they were an 'independent sect' in an even stricter sense than they are now; but it is rather an over-statement to say that they follow 'none' of the ordinary practices of Hinduism. To be sure, the Sadhs will not agree that any of theirs are Hindu customs, but the observer cannot help but notice the parallel.

The Origin of the Sadh Religion

Coming now to what the Sadhs themselves believe regarding the origin of their religion, it may be well, first of all, to list the incarnations believed in by the Sadhs.

Primitive Age (*Sat Yug*)

Govind and Parmeshwar	sons of	Mahadeo (Adam) and Parvati (Eve)

Second Age (*Dwapar Yug*)

Ram Chandar and Lakshman	successors to	Govind and Parmeshwar

Third Age (*Treta Yug*)

Krishna and Balbhadar	successors to	Lakshman and Ram Chandar

[1] The census of 1890.

[2] First edition, p. 74.

PRESENT AGE (*Kal Yug*)

Birbhan and Jogi Das	successors to	Krishna and Balbhadar

The first four pairs of names are all familiar names in Hinduism. Parmeshwar is a common name for God. It is generally used when referring to God in the abstract, that is apart from any representation in the form of an idol. Ram Chandar and Lakshman were brothers, the former being the hero of the famous Hindi classic, the *Ramayana*. Whether historical or not, Ram has been elevated to the place of a god. Krishna stands for what is highest and best in modern Hinduism, and is usually spoken of as Lord Krishna. It is only when we come down to the last two names, Birbhan and Jogi Das, that we find something distinctively Sadh. The Sadhs believe these two incarnations to have been historical, and to have been contemporaries of each other; and they look upon them as divine incarnations of equal prestige and importance. These two will be discussed in greater detail in Chapter II. The above list of names does not appear as a whole in the Sadh scriptures, although most of the names do appear individually here and there. The list was prepared and given to the writer by a group of leading Sadhs of Farrukhabad. Except for Birbhan and Jogi Das, the above named personages play little part in the practical religion of present-day Sadhs.

While the above-mentioned incarnations may be called the spiritual ancestors of Birbhan and Jogi Das, their progenitors in the physical sense are given in a table of twelve generations (*barah piri*).

The twelve generations:

1. Rawat Bhup	7. Hari Singh
2. Ram Singh	8. Girdhari Singh
3. Bakhtawar Singh	9. Moti Singh
4. Gokal Singh	10. Bagh Singh
5. Harmant Singh	11. Gopal Singh
6. Dhatar Singh	12. Jogi Das and Birbhan

Not only were Jogi Das and Birbhan contemporaries, but they were believed to be brothers in the flesh. Their mother was Jamanti or Jaivanti. The above table of the twelve generations is not found in Sadh sacred writings; but it is well-known to the better educated Sadhs, or rather to the more religiously inclined Sadhs. One is led to compare this list with that of the Ten Gurus who founded the Sikh Religion of the Punjab, though the names, of course, are different. Also it is not impossible to conceive a parallel between this genealogical table and the twelve disciples of Jesus.

The Sadh scriptures themselves have something to say about the early stages of the Sadh religion and history. Although these statements are probably of more interest and value to the student of comparative religion than to the historian, nevertheless they are regarded as authentic history by the orthodox Sadh. The following quotations are from the Sadhs' most sacred book, the *Nirvana Gyan.*

1

In Benares, Kabir's name was changed to Uda Das.

The name *Kabir* (Arabic, 'great') is one of the Muslim names for God. The best-known historical Kabir was a reformer who in the sixteenth century established a sect, extant today, known as the *Kabir Panth.* The Sadh religion has doubtless borrowed from Kabir's writings.

2

Having received the command, he built a house in Ellora.

Ellora, in the northern part of the Nizam's Dominions, is famous for its caves. The Sadhs believe that man was first created at Ellora, and incidentally that this 'first man' was a Sadh.

3

There were Sadhs in the First Period, Sadhs in the Second Period,
They became known in the Third Period,
In the Fourth Period (Kal Yug) there was a complete revelation.

This quotation proves to the orthodox Sadh that his race and religion have existed from the beginning of time. Jogi Das and Birbhan, in the present age, were the instruments of the 'complete revelation.'

4

The True Teacher has told me that you, a Brahman, ate goat-meat,
God says that whoever eats meat will go to hell.

This seems to mean that during the Third Age the Sadhs began to be known because they continued their practice of refusing to eat meat. In this matter they defied even the Brahmans.

CHAPTER II

THE DELHI SADHS

In this chapter an attempt is made to deal with the Sadhs in the neighbourhood of Delhi. This includes the community of Narnaul, seventy or seventy-five miles south-west of Delhi, the Rohtak Sadhs, about fifty miles north of Delhi, and various other places and groups within an equal radius. The places of most importance are as follows: Narnaul, Lalpur, Jaipur, Jodhpur, Muttra, Broda, Katwal, Ghilaur, Guhna, Rohut, Chiri, Rohna, Kawali, Rukhi, and Jind State.

The Punjab Gazetteer contains this brief statement:

> There are Satnami Sadhs found in the villages of Chiri, Ghilor, Kalan, and other villages. They are a sect of free-thinking Jats, whose founder was one Uda Das of Farrukhabad.[1]

The *Karnal District Gazetteer* contains the following statement:

> A peculiar sect known as Sadhs, and mostly of the Jat tribe, own villages of Zainpur, Sadhan and half of Garhi Sadhan in Indra *Pargana*. They are followers of Guru Udho Das, who was doubtless a reformer of the type of Kabir and Nanak. They worship no material object, paying no respect to the Jumna and Ganges. They have no temple or idol worship, only one God under the title of '*Sat*' or True One. They have a *gurudwara* in which the whole community meets on each *puranmasi* (full-moon), when precepts are recited. Music is prohibited. They neither 'fee' nor feed Brahmans, nor allow them to take any part in weddings or funerals. At marriages the *Phera* (circle) is presided over by a *Panch* (committee of five) of respectable Sadhs. Following the orders of the *guru* they salaam to no one but the Supreme Being. This peculiarity sometimes gets them into trouble with native officials.[2]

[1] Vol. III, Rohtak, 1910, p. 60.
[2] Edition of 1890, p. 91.

The Two Traditions

There are two traditions regarding the origin of the Sadhs. The first one we may call the Farrukhabad tradition. It was given to Mr. William Trant in 1827 by Bhawani Das Sadh of Farrukhabad, and runs as follows:

About the year 1600 of the era *Vicramaditya* (corresponding with A.D. 1544), a person named Birbhan, inhabitant of Birjasir (Bijesar), near Narnaul, in the province of Delhi, received a miraculous communication from Udaya Das, teaching him the particulars of the religion now professed by the Sauds (Sadhs). Udaya (Uda) Das, at the same time, gave to Birbhan marks by which he might know him at his reappearance:

1. That whatever he told should happen;
2. That no shadow should be cast from his figure;
3. That he should tell him his thoughts;
4. That he should be suspended between heaven and earth;
5. That he should bring the dead to life.[1]

Investigations by the present writer have proved that this tradition is held *in toto* by present day Sadhs of Farrukhabad. They make no claim that their religion had its inception in Farrukhabad.

The other tradition, which we may name the Delhi tradition, was reduced to writing by the Rev. Henry Fisher of Meerut, in 1818. The story was told to him by one Jai Singh Sadh, of the village of Kawali, District Rohtak, Punjab. It runs as follows:

About one hundred and sixty years ago, [A.D. 1818 *less* 160 equals A.D. 1658], Jogee (Jogi) Das, son of Gopal Singh of Bindair, when at an advanced age, had command of a body of troops in the service of the Raja of Doolpoor (Dholpur), and was slain in action with the enemies of this prince. His dead body was not suffered to remain neglected on the field of battle; but was miraculously recalled to life, as is pretended, by a stranger, in the habit of a mendicant; whose holy and venerable appearance excited in the mind of the astonished Jogee Das the deepest respect and confidence. The stranger led him away to the solitudes of a distant mountain and there detained him in the diligent study of those sacred truths which it was intended he should disseminate among the people. As soon as he was adjudged sufficiently qualified for the labours of his mission, the mendicant stranger returned him to his friends, with a commission to inculcate the doctrine which he had received. . . . From this period Jogee Das

[1] For Trant's complete article, see Chap. iv. Sadhs claim that these five points are in their holy book.

had many converts to his opinions, among his own immediate relatives and friends, and from among them he selected as his disciple one who should assist him in his labour to convert the people from idolatry to the worship of God as a Spirit, and with the heart and life. He chose Bheer Bhan (Birbhan) to attend him on a circuit, which he began to make in order to propagate his new opinions. . . . Jogee Das continued to propagate his tenets for twelve years.[1]

The Founders of the Sadh Religion

These two traditions are mixed up together as one tradition among the Sadhs. Both the Farrukhabad and Delhi groups hold to these details in the main. They have never studied them carefully enough to note any discrepancies. Thus three names are mentioned in connection with the founding of the Sadh religion: Uda Das, Jogi Das, and Birbhan. These three all appear in the Sadh scripture called, the *Nirvana Gyan*. The Sadhs claim that Jogi Das and Birbhan were brothers. The Farrukhabad tradition speaks of Uda Das and his successor, Birbhan; while the Delhi tradition speaks of Jogi Das and his successor, Birbhan. The Farrukhabad tradition gives the date as A.D. 1544; while the Delhi tradition gives it as A.D. 1658.

Were there then three persons, or two, and how many of them are historical? Birbhan is pretty generally accepted as a historical person. There is less evidence for the historicity of the other two. Professor J. N. Farquhar (assuming the historicity of all three) treats them in the following order: Uda Das, Birbhan, and Jogi Das.[2] The reference in the Delhi tradition to the battle of the army of the Raja of Dholpur is not to be found in any other sources. In this connection, Professor Jadu Nath Sarkar writes:

> I have not been able to find any mention of Jogi Das, as one of the founders of the Sadh sect in the Persian histories dealing with the war near Dholpur in 1658. The nearest approach I can trace to the Raja of Dholpur at the time is Maha Singh, Raja of Bhadawar (a place some miles east of Dholpur), who was a trusted general under Dara Shukoh and fought in the battle of Samugarh in 1659.[3]

The present writer offers the following thesis as a possible

[1] For Fisher's full account see Chap. iii.
[2] See his complete statement in Chap. v.
[3] In private correspondence with the writer.

solution of this historical problem. There may be only two persons involved, not three. These are Jogi Das and Birbhan. The name Uda Das is a title rather than a name. Its extensive use in the Sadh scriptures gives weight to this theory. 'Uda Das' appears in the *Nirvana Gyan* about one hundred and fifty times and sometimes is written 'Uda ke Das' (servant of God). It is apparently used by the writers to apply to both Jogi Das and Birbhan, but is more generally used as a title for the former. The two dates may be harmonized thus: the first date, A.D. 1544, is the approximate date of the career of Jogi Das, who was the founder of the sect, the leader of the revolt, and the establisher of the new cult. In other words, the Sadh religion in its popular form had its origin under Jogi Das about the middle of the sixteenth century. This is not too early a date to allow time for the influence of Kabir's teaching to spread, for Kabir died in A.D. 1518. The traditional story of the death of Jogi Das corresponds in many details with the story of Kabir's death, and was most probably composed by someone who was alive at the time of Kabir's death. The second date, A.D. 1658, we may accept as the approximate year of a new awakening of the adherents of this new faith. About this time their teachings were put into written form. By this date there had been time enough for Christian teachings to spread abroad, through the efforts of Father Busee, and other Jesuit Fathers, predecessors of Busee, who had been received in the courts of Akbar (1555–1605), of Jahangir (1605–27), of Shahjahan (1628–58).[1] This gave opportunity for Christian doctrine to have become well known, so that Birbhan and his followers could accept and include various elements of it in their own creed. This point will be taken up later. Further, it seems probable that (notwithstanding Sadh tradition to the contrary) Jogi Das and Birbhan were not brothers. It will be seen later that Dr. Farquhar puts Birbhan first and Jogi Das second.[2] The writer puts Jogi Das first and assigns a subsequent date to Birbhan, because of the tradition that Jogi Das was a fighting ascetic. If he was a fighter, it is most

[1] Sir Edward Maclagan, *The Jesuits and the Great Mogul*, 1932.

[2] See Chap. v.

unlikely that he was a literary man. We conclude then that Jogi Das, the fighter, brought the new faith into being, in a dramatic and popular manner; while Birbhan, the quiet student, crystallized the new faith and gave it standing among other sects of that age, by collecting and editing not only the contents of the Sadh holy book, but also a hymn book, the *Bani.* It may be said that the above theory does not harmonize with the assertion that Jogi Das was a fighter in the rebellious times of the second half of the seventeenth century. But in the absence of any authentic proof, it may be argued that fighting and petty warfare were probably the order of the day no less in the sixteenth than in the seventeenth century. In fact this very period under discussion (1540–50) was the time when Humayun, the supposed king of the land, was absent in Persia.

Contemporary History

The Satnami rebellion occurred in A.D. 1672, during the reign of Aurengzebe (1658–1707); and it was during the decade 1670–80 that the Satnami sect is believed to have had its origin. Although the Sadhs call themselves 'Sadh Satnami,' and among the villagers the one word 'Satnami' is commonly used, they are nevertheless not to be confused with the Satnami sect. In the expression 'Sadh Satnami,' the second word is a descriptive adjective and not the real name. No definite relation has been found between the Satnami sect and the Sadhs; but probably the fact that the word 'Satnami' has been used by both sects has led to confusion of the two. There is also the possibility that certain village groups of Satnamis were subsequently converted to the Sadh faith and retained their former name. This theory would account for village Sadhs being called 'Sadh-Satnami.'

The Satnami rebellion is mentioned by many historians of that period; and tales of miraculous powers and supernatural happenings among the followers of this new sect are told with much zeal by the contemporary historians of that time. It is not necessary to quote them here. Dr. Farquhar, after having made a careful study of the literature of that period, writes:

The only great fight with ascetics in the seventeenth century which I have as yet met in my reading took place in 1673, between a large mass of Satnami insurgents and a section of the army of Aurengzeb.[1]

In addition to this 'one great fight' there were doubtless numerous other engagements of a minor nature, throughout the whole duration of the Mogul dynasty.

In J. N. Sarkar's *History* we read:

The revolt of the Satnami *faqirs* in May, 1672 has gained a place in the history of Aurengzib out of all proportion to its size or political importance. Unlike other popular disturbances of the reign it appealed to the vulgar craze for the supernatural and sent a short thrill of fear through the capital itself.[2]

Our theory is that the Sadh religion was fairly well established before the rebellion of A.D. 1672 (or 1673); and hence that that particular insurrection played little or no part in influencing the account of the early history of the Sadhs. Present-day Sadhs strongly resent any reference which suggests any connection of their religious ancestors with the rather vulgar (and perhaps low-caste) fighters of the Satnami sect. The Sadh scriptures apparently contain no historical materials. At the request of the writer, the Farrukhabad Sadhs (with apparent sincerity) have searched through their *Nirvana Gyan*, but have found nothing of historical value. The names of Jogi Das and Birbhan appear, sometimes together, sometimes separately, and it is stated that these two men lived in the 'Present Age.' Except for the statement that Kabir's name was changed to Uda Das while he was at Benares, we find nothing that even approaches historical narrative in the Sadh holy book. It has been stated also by these same Sadh friends that not a single date of any chronological reckoning is to be found in the above mentioned scriptures.

Hence a continuous narrative concerning the Delhi Sadhs right down to the present day is obviously out of the question. A description of this more or less scattered community as it existed in the early part of the nineteenth century will be presented in the next chapter. For the present, omitting the

[1] *The Armed Ascetics of India.* (Unpublished.)
[2] J. N. Sarkar, *History of Aurengzib*, Vol. III, p. 295.

whole of the eighteenth century and leaving another large gap in the nineteenth century, we may come now to study the Sadhs of Delhi and Rohtak as they exist today. This material will be given in the form of travel-notes, gathered when the writer spent several days visiting these interesting people.

A Tour of the Rohtak Villages

These Sadh communities vary in size from two or three to twenty families. In some of the villages the leading men were not found at home. A few men and women had gone to the annual religious festival (*Bhandara*) at Farrukhabad. In most groups at least one literate man was to be found, and usually some of the boys were said to be reading in local schools.

No copies of the Sadh holy book were found in these villages; but some of them could name their scriptures, and several of them recognized quotations from it, when the same were read to them. Their neighbours call them Satnami rather than Sadh. In only one of the villages visited had there ever been a place of worship (*chauki*), and this had been allowed to tumble down.

In reply to the inquiry as to their identity, the common explanation given was: 'Our caste is Jat; our religion is Sadh.' They greet one another with the word '*Dandot*' (*Dhandawat*). The response to 'Dandot' is supposed to be 'Sat Guru'; but this term is not in common usage.

In one village a Government notice, dated April 1859, was shown to the writer, stating that Sadhs should not be required to salute by raising the hand to the forehead, as such a practice is against their religion.

An annual *mela* used to be held regularly in one or other of these villages, but for the past fifteen years or so it has been held in Farrukhabad and in other cities.

They marry their children to Hindu Jats. The head of the family or group serves the sacramental meal (*Prasad*) at each full-moon.

One group had been excommunicated for smoking; another group because (so the neighbours said) they had taken a man's ashes to the Ganges river for burial.

In most of the villages visited the Sadhs were found to be the most prosperous people of the village. Further mention of these village Sadhs will be found in the final chapter of this book.

CHAPTER III

AN 'AUTHENTIC ACCOUNT OF THE SAADHS'

BY

CHAPLAIN THE REV. HENRY FISHER OF MEERUT

[*The footnotes are inserted by the present writer*]

[THE Rev. Henry Fisher was a clergyman of the Church of England. After some years of service in a 'perpetual curacy,' he experienced a spiritual awakening. Soon after this new dedication of his life to more definitely spiritual pursuits, his thoughts were turned to India and its needs, by one Dr. Buchanan.

Arriving in India in 1815, Mr. Fisher served as a military chaplain for thirty years, until his death in Mussoorie, U.P., in 1845. From 1816 till 1832 he was stationed in Meerut, U.P., and during this period he not only performed his ordinary duties as a chaplain, but in addition he rendered great spiritual service to both European and Indian communities. He spent the last period of his service in Calcutta.

Chaplain Fisher soon acquired facility in speaking Hindustani; and in addition to his routine duties as an officer, he preached weekly at the Hindustani service. Within one year after his arrival in Meerut, we are told that high-caste Hindus were baptized as a result of his witness.

The *Missionary Register* states that in 1818 one of Mr. Fisher's Indian preachers had made 'the discovery of an extraordinary body of native Christians near Delhi.' This 'discovery' must have been made in the village of Kawali,[1] which was later named 'Henreepore,' in honor of Chaplain Henry Fisher. Further investigation revealed the fact that these so-called 'Christians' were none other than Sadhs, who had procured some copies of Henry Martyn's translations of the Gospels of Matthew and Mark.

In the Church Missionary Society magazine, the *Missionary Intelligence* (known after 1829 as *The Christian Intelligencer*) in the volume for 1825 we read:

'Joseph remains in Henreepore (Kawali) with the Sadh.' A Mission school had been opened there, and a strong effort was being made for

[1] The writer has visited this village. There are no Christians there today.

the complete evangelization of that Sadh group. Mr. Fisher's reports of these prospects aroused deep interest in missionary circles in England. One Sadh of Kawali was baptized in 1818; and hopes for the establishment of a Christian Church there were at their highest point in 1820. In 1824, Chaplain Fisher lamented the fact that he himself was not able to visit this remote village, in order that he might minister to the spiritual needs of the Sadhs and Christians. But from 1827 onwards, there is no further mention of Kawali in any missionary records.[1]

The following account indicates that Mr. Fisher had made careful and detailed inquiries into the history and tenets of the Sadhs. After much searching, the article[2] was finally discovered in London in 1925, by the late Dr. J. N. Farquhar.]

AN 'AUTHENTIC ACCOUNT OF THE SAADHS'[3]

'This sketch of the original and of the received opinions of the Saadhs (the virtuous) who have seceded from the Hindu idolatry, was obtained in two conversations from Jysingh,[4] the principal or headman of a division of the sect.

'About one hundred and sixty years ago, Jogee Das, son of Gopal Singh of Bindair, when at an advanced age, had command of a body of troops in the service of the Rajah of Doolpoor [Dholpur], and was slain in action with the enemies of this prince. His dead body was not suffered to remain neglected on the field of battle; but was miraculously recalled to life, as is pretended, by a stranger, in the habit of a mendicant; whose holy and venerable appearance excited in the mind of the astonished Jogee Das the deepest respect and confidence. The stranger led him away into the solitudes

[1] For further information, see Wilkinson's *Christianity in North India*, 1844, also Kaye's *Christianity in India*, 1859.

[2] Chaplain Fisher sent his account of the Sadhs to his friend, the Rev. Thomas Thomason of the Bible Society, Calcutta. It was published both in the *Missionary Intelligence*, 1818, and in the *C.M.S. Register*, London, in 1819. It was in the latter journal that Dr. Farquhar was able to locate it.

[3] The following note, evidently by the editor of the *Survey*, precedes the account: 'We refer our readers to page 32 of the *Survey* and here lay before them the account of the Saadhs which we there promised. It is contained in a letter from the Rev. Henry Fisher to the Rev. T. Thomason dated Meerut, 17 March, 1818: and affords much encouragement respecting these extraordinary peoples.'

[4] Of the village of Kawali; he was a subsequent convert, presumably in that very year.

of a distant mountain; and there detained him in the diligent study of those sacred truths which it was intended he should disseminate among the people, when he again returned into the world. As soon as he was judged sufficiently qualified for the labours of his mission, the mendicant stranger returned him to his friends, with a commission to inculcate the doctrines which he had received. His relatives and friends were astonished at his unexpected return and flocked round him with exclamations of surprise and joy, saluting him with their wonted phrase, "Ram, Ram!" "And who," he exclaimed, "is Ram?—O! understand and learn to know yourselves. The spirit now within me is no longer that of Jogee Das. Behold the testimony to the truth of my assertion." And, immediately addressing himself to a neighbouring neem tree, he caused it to utter articulate sounds familiar to their ears, and such expressions as had formerly been used by Jogee Das himself. After thus miraculously convincing them of the extraordinary powers which had been delegated to him, he proceeded to set before them the special object of his mission in words to the following effect: "I am sent to you by the *Sut Gooroo*" [*Sat Guru*] or True Pastor [Teacher], "to give you proper understanding and to deliver you from this ocean of error in which you are drowning." They prostrated themselves before him and kissed his feet. "Stop!" said he, "and hear me. Give all your heart to God. You are vexed by the Angel of Hell. Oh! wherefore will you remain thus blind! Receive light, and walk henceforth in the way of God. The place of rest is far off and the path of the world is difficult. He only who is strong and faithful can travel it. To overcome the wicked one is an arduous task: it is to walk on the edge of a sharp scimitar: therefore seat yourselves in the vessel of the knowledge of the Holy Teacher and you shall be transported beyond the disquieting waves." From this period Jogee Das had many converts to his opinions, among his own immediate relatives and friends, and from among them he selected as his disciple one who should assist him in his labour, to convert the people from idolatry to the worship of God as a Spirit, and with the heart and life. He chose Bheer Bhan [Birbhan] to attend him in a circuit which he began to make in order to propagate his new opinions. At each place where he met with success, it was his regular habit to find out, on his departure, one of the disciples whom he thought most worthy, to take charge of the young congregation to be left behind, as to discipline and moral conduct. At Delhi he appointed Sham Das; at Ajmeer, Bhooder Das; at Khamslee, Parisjee; at Munorpoor, Manajee; at Bhunondha, Gokul Das; and at Dadaree, Soondur Das. Jogee Das continued his itinerant labour, to propagate his tenets, for twelve years. He departed from this world at Bindee Su, without apprising his followers of his intention, in the following manner.

'Reclining himself upon the earth, after his usual custom, to repose for the night, he drew over him a large sheet and was supposed to be asleep. The following morning, however, on removing the sheet, he was no more to be seen; only the ground which his body had pressed was beautifully embellished with fresh and fragrant flowers.

'So much for the fabulous minglings in this narrative. The Saadhs appear to possess little or no learning, and very few speculative doctrines and, indeed, in the simplicity of their minds, hold out, as I conceive, the most inviting promise of successful labour of the Christian missionary. Their hearts are apparently prepared for such an effort in their favour by their present pre-disposition to spirituality of opinion in all that concerns the Supreme Being and the human soul. They profess to believe in one Invisible God who retains everything in His own sovereign power; is everywhere present and is infinitely merciful; and who, in proof of this exceeding disposition to mercy, sent or rather deputed the *Sut Gooroo* to enlighten and instruct poor ignorant men. This *Sut Gooroo*, who instructed Jogee Das (to whom also the Saadhs occasionally apply the same honorary title) in the knowledge of the truth, they esteem as the immediate *ċhela* or pupil of the Supreme Being.

'Is not this idea a probable legendary misrepresentation of the information communicated to the Saadhs, in the first instance, by Jogee Das who, if he was a Christian, as I think by no means improbable, would teach his disciples the doctrine of Christ's Divinity, of His being the True Shepherd, the only enlightened teacher of a pure spiritual religion and the free gift of mercy from God, suited to supply all the wants and miseries of sinful men? They also utterly exclude from their religious system all the Hindoo Deities, reject with abhorrence the use of images and hold the Incarnations of Vishnoo to have been Conquerers, or some disinterested and famous Benefactors of mankind, by whom they have been idolatrously exalted into the seat of God. They consider pilgrimages as folly; and have no faith whatever in the efficacy of ablutions, neither do they practise them at all, except for the purpose of cleanliness. Jysingh [Jai Singh] smiled very significantly on being asked what he thought of the Ganges and the Jumna. He said that they were very useful rivers, and should be considered merely as objects of notice whereby to call to mind the goodness of God. They do not receive the doctrine of transmigration or pretend to any authentic knowledge of the creation of the world. They fully expect a future judgment which will establish the virtuous and holy in a state of uninterrupted happiness; but will doom the wicked to dreadful torments, whereby they shall expiate their sins which they have committed in the world. The duration of the punishment of the condemned will, however, be increased by the nature and provocation of their respective crimes, and eternal happiness will be the final issue of all things. The *Sut Gooroo* will be visibly present at the great Day of Account; but they do not seem to anticipate any benefit from his intercession in their behalf, or to have any notice of atonement but that of their own sufferings. For divine worship they have no temple, but a hut called *Jumlu Ghur* [evidently this means *Jama ghar*, i.e. assembly house] usually situated in the village where the elder or principal of a congregation may happen to reside.

'Jogee Das arranged for his people that they should meet weekly on Saturdays; on which day they were to lay aside all kind of labour, and in the ensuing night to pass the hours in religious meditation, in praise of and prayer to God. The Saadhs, however, being principally poor labouring men, hardly bestead for daily bread, found that so frequent an interruption to their means of support for themselves and families could not be conveniently submitted to; and therefore, in due course of time, a monthly meeting was substituted for their former weekly one, and now they assemble only on the day of every full moon.

'The simplicity of this meeting is very interesting; and cannot but strike us with its similarity in some respects to our sacramental feast. The whole of the Saadhs who reside at a convenient distance, females included, assemble at the nearest *Jumlu Ghur*; each person furnishing, according to his means, flour, ghee, milk or sugar. Part of the congregation is employed during the day in making these materials into bread; while others converse on the affairs of the community, or investigate any complaints that may be brought forward against their people. In the evening the bread is placed upon a small elevation in the *Jumlu Ghur* [house of worship] and after a short extempore prayer, is divided among the guests. A vessel containing ***sharbet***, called a cup of fellowship, is also passed round; and the remainder of the night is spent in rehearsing verses in praise of the *Sut Gooroo* and listening to the legendary stories of their founder and directions for their moral conduct in life.

'Any member convicted of immorality is precluded from participating in their food or associating in their worship. Excommunication is their special punishment; the duration of this discipline being wholly regulated by and proportioned to the atrocity of the offence.

'Besides these monthly meetings of the various district divisions there is a general annual assembly in the month of March; the spot determined by its local convenience. Last year it took place in Delhi; at the time when Anund[1] met with them, in *tope*, or groce [*sic*]: and this year they will assemble at Futtyguth [Fatehgarh].[2] The business of this public meeting corresponds with that of the monthly—their special object being to canvass the moral interests of the whole party and to investigate the conduct of the different members.

'The Saadhs have no regular order of priesthood. That man who, in each particular division, happens to be consi-

[1] Anund Masih was a convert of Mr. Fisher's. He first told Chaplain Fisher about this unusual community.

[2] Fatehgarh is modern spelling. The place is in the district of Farrukhabad, U.P. The Sadhs live in Farrukhabad, not in Fatehgarh.

dered most respectable, who can read, repeat the hymns, and relate their traditions, is constituted their chief, though always with limited authority. Their moral precepts seem to be of an excellent character; forbidding falsehood, dishonesty, and all dissolute practices and flagitious actions. They are directed to earn their living by honest industry and are never to eat the bread of idleness or to receive presents.

'Their nuptial rite is simple; all unnecessary expense being scrupulously avoided. Polygamy is never allowed and even widows are forbidden to unite with second husbands; while persons of different trades intermarry without the least hesitation, there being no difficulty in taking a wife from any with whom an agreement can be made.

'As they are taught to esteem the soul the immortal part of man and as the greatest value, they have no prescribed mode of disposing of their dead. Formerly, the bodies were cast into the jungle to be devoured by wild beasts; to this succeeded the practice of interment; at present, they usually consume them with fire, or cast them into the adjacent rivers. When on their way to the funeral pile or rivers to dispose of their dead, instead of the words pronounced by Hindoos—"Ram, Ram, Sulhum" [Salam]—they substitute, "Attend to your devotions." They know nothing of any rites for the repose of the departed soul; but believe that it is either happy or miserable according to its conduct while in the body, and that at the future great day of judgment body and soul will be united.

'Much anxiety prevails among them respecting a due preparation for this awful day of judgment; but their present, indeed their only stay, seems to be derived from their own devotional exercises: and when their consciences are distressed through falls into sin their consolations are drawn from the same source, trusting that they will secure (if accompanied by strong determination never again to do what they ought not to do) complete reconciliation with God. The conviction upon their minds seems settled that a rigid performance of their several duties will certainly secure them future happiness; and yet, with much apparent humility they acknowledge themselves sinners.

'Books appear to be very scarce among the Saadhs. Jysingh

has with him two small ones, containing fabulous stories and songs in verse. They are ill transcribed in the common Nagree character and the paper much worn. The language is the current one of the Hindus, having very few Arabic or Persian words. They make no pretence that these books contain the writings of Jogee Das. Any Saadh believing himself to be under the influence of the same Divine Spirit which they suppose to have inspired their first founder, is at perfect liberty to offer his own productions at their religious assemblies for public repetition; and so long as they are moral, and not in contradiction to their received opinions, they will not be objected to.[1]

'A tradition obtains credit among them that, after a lapse of thirteen years according to the calculation, the *Shudh-Sut*[2] will rapidly increase and that eventually the whole population of Hindoostan will embrace their tenets. When a Hindoo, no matter what his caste may be, is disposed to become a convert, he is expected to submit himself implicitly to the guidance and instruction of an experienced Saadh for a considerable time. If in the course of this probationary trial, just reason shall appear to approve his motives and his conduct, he is publickly presented with a cup of cold water, a draught from which constitutes him a Saadh. He still retains his own name; but is thenceforward admitted into the fellowship of their communion.

'The Saadhs are very scrupulous concerning meats, eat no animal flesh, drink no spirits and will only receive water from the hands of a Saadh. They dress like the Hindoos, the men always wearing a white turban. The Hindoos generally seem to know very little about these people, and indeed to everybody to whom I have mentioned them they appear quite a new object of interest and attention. They have been erroneously supposed to be a branch of the Joinus.[3] It is evident that the Saadhs are familiarly acquainted with the numbers and places of residence of their people; so that

[1] It is noticeable that among the religious leaders of the Sadhs, there is a general tendency to want to write something.

[2] i.e. conversion to the truth, a sort of technical term.

[3] The Jains. This idea arose from the fact that Sadhs consider even the life of an insect as sacred.

a frequent intercourse among them probably takes place. Jysingh from memory mentioned about thirty villages and particularized the various families of each place.[1] In the direction of Bengal, there are not, so far as he can tell, any Saadhs below Mirzapore.[2] He has heard that some few are to be found in the Deccan [South] but cannot speak with any certainty.

'Three or four years ago (Anund heard in the Tope, five or six[3]) a copy or two of the Serampore translation of some of the Gospels were brought from Hurdwan [Hardwar] by some of their persuasion, who had visited the Fair. Of the spirit, or proper meaning of the contents, however, they knew very little, till, about ten months ago, some passages were read to them and explained by Anund Messeeh. At first a good deal of superstitious apprehension deterred them from meddling with religious matters; a fanciful persuasion also having taken possession of their minds that if they should show any willingness to listen to Christian instruction, we should in propagating our tenets use like instruments and means with Mahomedans, for whom they retain a rooted antipathy.[4] As they have, however, obtained information, their prejudices are considerably abated; so much so indeed, that they are very ready to receive and use our books and to listen to Anund's comments. Jysingh stated his readiness to undertake with assistance to read to, and to teach to read, the children of the Saadhs; who are all very anxious to learn to read and write, whenever any opportunity presents itself. Jysingh is also of opinion and indeed has no doubt that many Saadhs will attend when leisure from their agricultural or other pursuits will allow, to hear the Gospels read; as in some places, where they have the books, has been already done.

'In consequence of these communications (the whole of which I had great pleasure in laying before Mr. Metcalf, and who himself conversed a good deal with Anund and with

[1] This is true of present day Sadhs.

[2] In the Eastern part of the United Provinces.

[3] This was either a mistake in the original printing; or a later one by the London typist.

[4] This seems strange, since these people are followers of Kabir who was as much Muslim as he was Hindu.

Jysingh[1]) our new friend[2] was engaged to set about the enlightenment of the school in the village of Kowaly [Kawali], where he resides; I undertaking to send Anund to assist him in the outset; and purposing to be guided by circumstances as to its continuance in the future. On Anund's arrival, in the first week of January, he found that Jysingh, true to his engagements, had commenced his little school. It was, however, but poorly attended, there being only seven young children, daily scholars, who learned the alphabet, tracing the letters with their fingers in the sand; but when evening affords leisure and opportunity, by respite from their labours, both Saadhs and Jats assemble to the amount of thirty men and children to hear the old Saadhs read aloud a chapter from the Gospels; after which they generally apply themselves to learn their own mode of multiplication. The *Tumeendu*[3] of Kowaly, a Jat, has given a shed for their assemblies.

'Anund informs us that the opening of the school was considered an important event. To ensure it prosperity and permanency, the inhabitants had previous to Anund's arrival consulted an astrologer that the commencement of the school might be under the auspices of a happy conjunction. He fixed the twenty-seventh of December last.[4] Some Brahmins in the neighbourhood have expressed displeasure; considering the selection of the Saadhs as teachers to the seclusion and neglect of themselves as a very unfair and ill-judged preference; since the communication of the rudiments should, in their opinion, have remained their exclusive prerogative. It is not improbable that the strange opinions which have been propagated in the immediate neighbourhood of Kowaly and the adjacent villages have their origin in the dissatisfaction and consequent misrepresentation of these Brahmins: some of the people having taken up an idea that unworthy and interested motives have prompted this plan of education; and that, so soon as the children may be found qualified for their destined occupation and employment, the parents will be forcibly

[1] The reference to Mr. Metcalf has not been traced.

[2] i.e. Jai Singh, the literate Sadh who later was baptized.

[3] 'Tumeendu' must be 'Karinda,' i.e. the representative of a landlord in a village of tenants.

[4] This must have been the year 1818.

deprived of them. Time, however, will show the folly of such imaginations. In the meanwhile we try to go quietly forward.

'As Anund has been repeatedly cautioned not to let his warm imagination delude him into any exaggerated representations of what he may deem worth observing and communicating, I have no hesitation in believing this statement.'[1]

Comment on Mr. Fisher's Paper

The above account by Mr. Fisher is a valuable piece of research. Not only is it first-hand information, but also his investigations were one hundred years less remote from the date of the origin of the Sadh religion than any effort the present writer has been able to make.

On the other hand, Fisher's main motive was clearly not that of scientific research, but rather that of missionary propaganda for the home constituency, and also that of a preliminary step to evangelization of the Sadh community. Even if he had possessed the modern sympathetic attitude toward other religions (a rare thing in those days), still he would be handicapped in his efforts by the lack of opportunity to check his findings. He says that he had had only two conversations with Jai Singh at the time of writing his paper.

It is obvious that his paper is marked by a rather strong bias. Before ever meeting the Sadhs, he had been led to believe they were Christians; and that Jogi Das, one of the founders of Sadhism, was a Christian. This undoubtedly led Mr. Fisher to read into Sadh doctrines Christian elements which were probably not there. Yet it is only fair to recognize that most of the features which he interpreted as Christian may actually have been so; and the fact that they appear to be less so today may be due to further changes which have occurred in the Sadh religion in the last century. Therefore we do not mean to deny the Christian influence and possible Christian origin of some of the Sadh tenets, but we would only suggest that Fisher seems to have overstated the case in favour of Christian influence.

[1] One wonders whether Mr. Fisher did not experience disillusionment at some subsequent date.

Fisher is right in asserting that Sadhs 'have few speculative doctrines.' This is true today of village Sadhs, but less true of urban Sadhs, who have unconsciously reinstated several Hindu elements in their creed.

Jogi Das was most probably not a Christian, but may have been as much Christian as he was either orthodox Hindu or Muslim.

Their former custom of weekly meetings is almost certainly derived from Christianity. Indeed the Farrukhabad Sadhs used to meet on Sundays, but modern tendencies have led them to give up that custom almost entirely.

CHAPTER IV

THE FARRUKHABAD SADHS

[William Henry Trant, of Danish descent, was born in Ireland, and entered the Bengal Civil Service in 1798. In March, 1816, he visited the Sadhs of Farrukhabad, U.P. He may at that time have been stationed in Fategarh, the civil station of Farrukhabad District. After leaving India in 1824, he read a paper on the Sadhs before the Royal Asiatic Society in London, 5 February, 1825, and in 1827 this monograph was published in the *Transactions of the Royal Asiatic Society*. In 1828, Mr. Trant was elected to Parliament for Dover and in 1831 he became Member of Parliament for Oakhampton Borough. He died in 1859 or 1860. Mr. Trant's article is given below, as copied by the present writer from the *Transactions of the Royal Asiatic Society*, Vol. I, pp. 251 ff.]

'A SHORT ACCOUNT OF THE SADHS'

'BY WILLIAM HENRY TRANT, ESQ.

[*The footnotes are inserted by the present writer*]

'In March, 1816, I went with two other gentlemen from Fatahghar [Fategarh], on the invitation of the principal persons of the Saud [Sadh] sect, to witness an assemblage of them, for the purpose of religious worship, in the city of Farrukhabad, the general meeting of the sect for that year being there.

'The assembly took place within the courtyard of a large house, where the number of men, women and children was considerable. We were received with great attention; and chairs were placed for us in front of the hall. After some time, when the place was quite full of people, the ceremony commenced, which consisted simply in the chanting of a hymn; this being the only mode of public worship used by the Sauds.

'At subsequent periods I made particular inquiries relative

to the religious opinions and practices of this sect, and I was frequently visited by Bhawani Das, the principal person of the sect in the city of Farrukhabad. The following is the substance of the account given by Bhawani Das of the origin of this sect.

'About the year 1600 of the era of Vicramaditya (corresponding with A.D. 1544), a person named Birbhan, inhabitant of Birjasir [Bijaser] near Narnual, in the Province of Delhi, received a miraculous communication from Udaya Das, teaching him the particulars of the religion now professed by the Sauds. Udaya Das, at the same time, gave to Birbhan marks by which he might know him at his reappearance:

'1. That whatever he told should happen.
'2. That no shadow should be cast from his figure.
'3. That he should tell him his thoughts.
'4. That he should be suspended between heaven and earth.
'5. That he should bring the dead to life.

'Bhawani Das gave me a copy of the *Pothi*, or religious book of the Sauds, written in a kind of verse in the *T'henth* (vulgar) Hindi dialect; and he fully explained to me the leading points of their religion. That book I have now the honor to present to the Royal Asiatic Society.[1]

'The Sauds utterly reject and abhor all kinds of idolatry; and the Ganges is considered by them not to be a sacred object; although the converts are made chiefly, if not entirely, from among the Hindus, whom they resemble in outward appearance.

'Their name for God is *Satcara*,[2] and *Saud*, the appellation of the sect, means they say, 'Servant of God.'[3] They are pure deists; and their form of worship is most simple, as I have already stated. The Sauds resemble Quakers, or Society of Friends in England, in their customs in a remarkable degree. Ornaments and gay apparel of every kind are strictly prohibited. Their dress is always white. They never make

[1] This book cannot now be traced. Sadhs say it was not their real Scripture, but another book.

[2] This must be meant for 'Sat Guru' the True Teacher.

[3] They probably gave this as the meaning of 'Uda Das.' Sadh comes from 'Sadhu,' meaning a holy man.

any obeisance or salutation. They will not take an oath; and they are exempted in the courts of justice; their asseveration, like that of the Quakers, being considered equivalent.

'The Sauds profess to abstain from all luxuries; such as tobacco, betel, opium and wine. They never have exhibitions of dancing. All violence to man or beast is forbidden, but in self-defence resistance is allowable. The Sauds, like the Quakers, take great care of their poor and infirm people. To receive assistance out of the sect or tribe would be reckoned disgraceful, and render the offender liable to excommunication. All parade of worship is forbidden. Private prayer is commended. Alms should be unostentatious; they are not to be given that they may be seen of men. The due regulation of the tongue is a principal duty.

'The chief seats of the Saud sect are Delhi, Agra, Jayapur [Jaipur] and Farrukhabad; but there are several of the sect scattered over other parts of the country. An annual meeting takes place at one or other of the cities above mentioned at which the concerns of the sect are settled. In Farrukhabad the number was about three thousand.[1]

'The Magistrate of Farrukhabad informed me that he had found the Sauds an orderly and well-conducted people; they are chiefly engaged in trade. Bhawani Das was anxious to become acquainted with the Christian religion, and I gave him some copies of the New Testament in Persian and Hindustani[2] which he afterwards told me he had read and shown to his people, and much approved.

'I had no copy of the Old Testament in any language which he understood well; but as he expressed a strong desire to know the account of creation as given in it, I explained it to him from an Arabic version, of which language he knew a little.[3] I promised to procure him a Persian or Hindustani Old Testament[2] if possible.'

[1] Three thousand must have been an estimate and not an enumeration. The number was probably less than that.

[2] He evidently means Persian and Roman-Urdu.

[3] One wonders why he did not make his scriptural explanation in English or Hindustani.

A further introduction to the Farrukhabad community is given in the pages of the Farrukhabad *Gazetteer*:

They [Sadhs] are Unitarians, worshipping one God, the Author of the universe under the name of *Satya Guru*, or *Satya Nam*, and permitting no material representation of him of any kind. Their religion forbids them either to tell a lie or to take an oath, and they are prohibited from using any kind of drug or intoxicant. Adults are supposed to wear a white dress but no caste marks are allowed. Almost all the community is concentrated in the city of Farrukhabad where they occupy almost exclusively one of the city muhallas, the 'Sadhwara.' There are elsewhere Sadhs who till the soil, but here they are townsfolk pure and simple. The cloth-printing industry is entirely in their hands, and the richer members of the community are bankers and merchants, while some are large landowners. The poorer are traders and artisans. Connection with the other colonies of Sadhs is maintained by annual gatherings of the sect, held in turn at its various centres. Sadhs wear a distinctive headgear consisting of a round hard white hat like an inverted bowl, and their customary salute is performed by holding both hands with the palms outwards.[1]

Events Contemporary with the Origin of the Sadhs

Farrukhsiyar, the second successor of Aurengzeb, ruled the decaying Mogul kingdom from 1713 till 1719. He sent his minister, Muhammed Khan, to lay out the city of Farrukhabad, the new city being named in honour of King Farrukhsiyar. Mr. William Irvine, a local historian, tells us that the new city of Farrukhabad was founded December 27th, 1714.[2] The *Imperial Gazetteer* states that Muhammed Khan was a Bangash Afghan Nawab of Kaimganj, near Farrukhabad. 'He brought twelve thousand men to Farrukhsiyar in his contest for the throne, and was rewarded by a grant in Bundelkhand. In 1714 he obtained a grant near his own home and founded Farrukhabad.'[3]

At the very time the city was founded, one of its many quarters was named Sadhwara. William Irvine is responsible for the statement that:

Other quarters were set aside for peculiar castes, such as Khatranat Mochinana, Koliana, Sadhwara, for Sadhs. . . . This arrangement,

[1] p. 70.
[2] Wm. Irvine, I.C.S., *History of Farrukhabad*, 1713–1897 (Urdu).
[3] Vol. XII, 1908, p. 64.

is still observed to some extent. I doubt if a single Sadh lives outside of the Sadhwara and its offshoot, Sahibganj.[1]

There can be no doubt that Sadhs were quite numerous in Farrukhabad city as early as A.D. 1714.

THE FARRUKHABAD TRADITION

In trying to account for their settlement in Farrukhabad, local Farrukhabad Sadhs hold this tradition, that one of their ancestors was so greatly trusted by the Emperor Farrukhsiyar (they probably mean Muhammed Khan) that he was made manager of the local mint. Farrukhsiyar who was a noted coin-maker, had several mints, one of which was located in Farrukhabad.[2]

Professor C. J. Brown (the author of *The Coins of India*, in the 'Heritage of India' series) writes: 'I have a coin dated 1716 (one of Farrukhsiyar's); the Sadhs have always been bankers and merchants, and nothing is more likely than that one of them should have taken the contract for the new mint in Farrukhabad.'[3] The term *Taksaria* (Persian, 'coiner') has for generations been associated with one of the Sadh families of Farrukhabad. The older men of today still point out the place where the *Taksaria* used to live.

Another tradition (which, by the way, can be harmonized with the one above), runs as follows: The Sadhs, always a pacific people, were intentionally located by Muhammed Khan between two groups of pugnacious Muslims, namely the Khotak and Bangash, in the hope that the Sadhs would be the instruments of preserving the peace. In addition to this important service, we are told, their situation on the side of the city towards the Ganges river enabled them to defend their neighbours from the attacks of any robbers who might approach by way of the river. In those days, before the invention of the steam engine and the advent of the railway, the river was a highway of travel and commerce. The second part of this tradition seems to indicate that the Sadhs (or

[1] Journal Asiatic Society of Bengal, Vol. XLVII, Part I. p. 280. Wm. Irvine, I.C.S., *Bangash Nawabs of Farrukhabad*.

[2] C. J. Brown, *Coins of India*, pp. 92–106 (Y.M.C.A Publishing House).

[3] In private correspondence.

Hindus) became the buffer between the robber enemies and the Muslim dwellers of the city.

The writer believes that neither of the above traditions fully explains the story, nor do both together provide a satisfactory solution. These traditions may rather be considered as incidents in the gradual development of the Farrukhabad Sadhs; that is, in their transformation from rural Sadhs into urban Sadhs. The first converts to the Sadh religion in the United Provinces most certainly were villagers. Present-day Sadhs name three or four village communities from which their ancestors came. One family claims that their ancestors came from Etah; another (in fact, several others) say that they were originally from Kaimganj; others again claim connections with some villages near Kanauj. Gradually, as the desire for wealth became their ambition, and as opportunity offered, they left their ploughs and cows and joined forces with their prosperous co-religionists in Farrukhabad.

The Farrukhabad Sadhs

The next glimpse we get of the Farrukhabad Sadhs is in the year 1816, when Mr. Trant visited them.[1] Long before that time they had become a stable permanent community.

Swami Dayananda Sarasvati, founder of the Arya Samaj, paid six or seven visits to the Farrukhabad Sadhs, during the formative period of his life, that is, from about 1845 till 1860. He was evidently desirous of learning whether the Sadh religion could satisfy his troubled and hungry soul. The Sadhs relate how, on the occasion of one of the Swami's visits, an attack was perpetrated upon him by some city Hindus. The story goes that the nefarious scheme was frustrated by one of his Sadh friends.

In 1859, the Farrukhabad Sadhs were the object of the following official statement, to be found in the court records of Farrukhabad District:

> The Sadhs are a race peculiar to this part of the country, and by their religion are prohibited from making the usual 'salam,' but have

[1] See above, p. 30.

a form of their own of merely raising their hands. This note is given, as many of their caste have been beaten by officers lately, who were unacquainted with the nature of their religion.[1]

This indicates a willingness to suffer persecution in the name of religion.

In 1860, the house of worship (*chauki*) was erected. The date is written on the edifice. The construction of such a large building speaks of religious zeal, which must have been accompanied too by worldly prosperity. In the decade 1870–80, the local American missionaries cultivated the acquaintance of the Farrukhabad Sadhs; and, indeed, some evangelistic effort was made on their behalf. Further reference to this mission work will be found in Chapter XI.

The year 1875 marked the beginning of the cotton-printing industry among the Sadhs. The grandfathers of the present generation established the business which has developed into such a remunerative occupation.

In 1893, a young Sadh and his grandmother (or aunt) were baptized. This event created quite a furore among the Sadhs, so much so that in order to restore quiet the new converts were sent elsewhere.

In 1897, two Sadh merchants were received by Her Majesty Queen Victoria, in Buckingham Palace. Her Majesty had been informed beforehand regarding their peculiar manner of salutation.[2]

The early years of the present century witnessed a rather serious division in the Farrukhabad community of Sadhs. Umrau Singh Sadh[3] says it originated over a difference of opinion as to the manner of salutation. He writes: 'One party salutes only the Creator, while the other party salutes its fellow-men.' An extended court case accentuated the unpleasant affair. Judgment in this case was finally rendered in July, 1906. Jealousy and hatred apparently increased, and brought the issue to its climax in 1909. At that time, an official investigation was instituted by the

[1] Signed April 11, 1859, L. V. MacAndrew, Bridg. (In Fatehgarh Library.)

[2] *Prabha*, March, 1920. Sumer Chand Sadh and Sindar Chand Sadh, both living in 1930.

[3] Barthol-basi, to distinguish him from another of the same name.

District Magistrate of Farrukhabad; a report was made and a decision was rendered which brought the two parties together to accept an amicable agreement.[1] Years, however, passed before the fires of hatred and animosity, kindled during those bitter years, died out; but now the writer has been assured that the last vestige of the quarrel has happily disappeared.

Literacy among Farrukhabad Sadhs

The Farrukhabad Sadhs have a higher percentage of literacy than is to be found among the village Sadhs. Hindi is their mother tongue; while the village Sadhs north of Delhi speak Punjabi. The city Sadhs aspire to a good knowledge of business and conversational English. But they have not kept their sons in school long enough to pass college examinations for degrees. The above mentioned Umrau Sing Sadh has done a little writing in Hindi. During the troublous times of the factional dispute, he started a Hindi weekly newspaper,[2] apparently for the purpose of educating his caste brothers in the Sadh religious tenets. This paper was discontinued after six months, for the editor found that such a small community could not support a denominational paper. A copy of this short-lived paper, which is in the hands of the writer, contains not only an article on the Sadh creed, but also an editorial on the question at that time uppermost in the minds of all Sadhs, namely the division. In regard to the official document which brought to a close this unfortunate bit of history, we read:

> The excellency of the order lies in the fact that it does not infringe upon any of the principles of the Sadh religion.

The House of Worship

This chapter may well close with a description of the Farrukhbad house of worship. It is called *Chauki* (Hindi, 'seat,' 'station'). The entire compound where the building stands is about one acre. There are two outside gates. The

[1] Signed by A. W. MacNair, Magistrate, 26 February, 1909.
[2] *Sadh Susamachar* (Sadh Good-news).

general appearance of the whole place is that of an oriental *sarai.* One small building, standing alone, resembles a Hindu temple, and probably was built as such, but now it is quite devoid of any images. There is a large open space where tents are pitched at the time of large gatherings. Stored away in houses are to be found cooking utensils, and ample equipment for providing food for a multitude of visitors. Here and there are seats and trees, giving the whole place something of the appearance of a small park.

The *chauki* proper is a large building. It measures about fifty feet square and is quite forty feet high. There is but one entrance. The visitor is required to remove his shoes before entering. Inside are three rooms, so to speak, separated by arches and colonnades. Above are one small room and a roof garden. In this upper room, there is a small door in the wall, kept closed by means of a padlock. The writer was informed that this lock secures in safety the Sadh holy book, the *Pothi.* (Pothi is the Hindi-Sanskrit for 'book.') The special name for their book is *Nirvana Gyan.* In this private place the book is protected from the 'vulgar gaze of unbelievers.' The house is open at all times to all members of the sect. At almost any time the older men may be seen sitting in groups, or individually, in meditation. But the most commonly used place of worship is another place, a verandah quite separate from this presumably dedicated building.

The *chauki* is built of ordinary materials, has no special architectural beauty, and in fact was evidently erected without much special consideration of its unique use. There are no decorations, no rugs, no furniture, nothing to suggest idolatry, nothing to appeal to any of the emotions. It is a haven of rest where those so inclined may seek God in their own way. Over the entrance is the following inscription in Hindi:[1]

1. *Smaran karna*—Remember [God].
2. *Bura karna se dur rahna*—Abstain from all evil.
3. *Achchhe Sadhon ki rit par chalna*—Follow the customs of all good Sadhs.

The first precept is the second of the nine forms of worship believed in by orthodox Hindus. The second is a

[1] Translations by the present writer.

maxim common to all religions. The third one suggests that the faith of their fathers should be accepted by all Sadhs without doubt or question. Over the above three precepts is this sentence in Nagri character:

'In this place three things are taught; discourse and argument are forbidden.' The practical way by which the Sadhs avoid 'discourse and argument' in the church is to have their meetings in another place, as explained above.

In this same compound is a marble slab, a memorial to some departed Sadh, one of whose names was Nanak. Nanak was one of the founders of the Sikh religion, elements of which, as we shall later see, are to be found in the Sadh religion.

CHAPTER V

THE RECONSTRUCTION OF SADH HISTORY

By the late Dr. J. N. Farquhar

[*The footnotes are inserted by the present writer*]

[Among recent scholars no one has contributed more to our knowledge of the Sadhs than Dr. J. N. Farquhar. Born in 1861, as a lad he served his apprenticeship as assistant in a large drapery shop in Aberdeen; and from there, he secured a bursary to the University of Aberdeen; and in 1885, an Exhibition to Christ Church, Oxford. He achieved an honourable career in both universities, securing a 'double first' at Oxford.

In 1891 he came out to India as a missionary of the L.M.S., and was stationed at Calcutta, first as an evangelistic missionary, and afterwards as the head of the L.M.S. Institution in Bhowanipur. After twelve years' service with the L.M.S., in 1902 he accepted the invitation to join the staff of the Indian Y.M.C.A., and was for some years Secretary in charge of the Y.M.C.A. student branch in College Street, Calcutta. In 1912, he was appointed by the Y.M.C.A as the first National Secretary of its Literature Department; and for the next eleven years he devoted himself unwearyingly to this work. It was through his energy and foresight that the Association Press (Y.M.C.A.) undertook the publication of the various series of books which have now come to be so closely associated with Dr. Farquhar's name; and nearly fifty volumes altogether were published by the Association Press under Dr. Farquhar's leadership.

Dr. Farquhar was not only an editor and publisher, but also a reader and scholar; and before he left India he had won for himself a recognized place as one of the foremost living authorities on the religious life and traditions of India. He retired from India in 1923, and during the last years of his life was Professor of Comparative Religion in the University of Manchester. He died at Manchester on July 17th, 1929.

The writer has a large file of Dr. Farquhar's letters, all of which deal with the Sadhs.

The following historical statement by Dr. Farquhar was prepared by him after he had taken up his duties at Manchester University. It is based on what Dr. Farquhar already knew of the Sadhs, supplemented by a careful study of all the new materials which the present writer was able to gather for him.—Ed.]

I. THE HIGHER HINDUISM.[1]

'Until the appearance of the *Bhagavadgita* (probably in the first century A.D.) Hinduism had been frankly polytheistic. There were numerous sects, each claiming that its divinity was the greatest of the gods, but that was all. In the Upanishads we are taught that the One, the Brahman, the Atman, the source of the universe, of all gods and all men, exists, but that he is impersonal, unknowable, beyond reach of praise and prayer. He is thus a pantheistic, impersonal Supreme, standing in no relation to practical religion. Sannyasis sought to find release by meditation on him; but no one attempted to worship him.

'In the *Gita*, Krishna, who was the god of one of the chief sects, says that he himself is the Brahman; and his sect accepted the statement. Thus, from this time onward, the sect thought of itself as having the Brahman of the universe for its god; and, being identified with Krishna, the Brahman was naturally regarded by the sect as personal. Thus we have here a very distinct advance in the direction of theism. Unfortunately, they still recognized the existence of all the other Hindu gods, conceived Krishna as having many consorts, and continued to practise idol-worship.

'Naturally, every other noteworthy sect made a similar claim for its god. Thus Hinduism consisted in the main, for centuries, of a dozen great sects, each claiming for its own god the position of the Supreme, yet each recognizing the existence of all the other gods, and using idols. Thus we have here no real monotheism but an advanced idolatrous polytheism, with a dozen leading gods each clamouring for the chief place, yet each conceived as having many consorts and children and as living in heaven with all the other gods. This is clearly not monotheism, but polytheism with a most imperfect theistic idea, held by a dozen warring sects.[2]

'Kabir (*c.* A.D. 1440–1518) seems to have been brought up as a Muhammadan; but, while he was still a boy, he came under the influence of Ramananda and accepted from him a

[1] This section shows the evolution from polytheistic idolatry towards spiritual monotheism.

[2] See *The Crown of Hinduism*, Chap. viii.

good deal of Hindu thought. At a later date, he became an independent teacher, and taught an amalgam of Hinduism and Islam. He is definitely a monotheist and will have nothing to do with idolatry, but he taught the doctrine of transmigration and *karma*, and is thus a Hindu. From his influence arose the Sikhs and ten other theistic groups. Rai Das, the Chamar, who was also a disciple of Ramananda,[1] taught Kabir's system, as is plain from many passages in the Sikh Granth;[2] and Uday Das was a disciple of Rai Das. Hence the teaching given by Birbhan, who was a disciple of Uday Das, would be practically the same as the teaching of Kabir.

II. Reconstruction of Sadh History

'Now the Sadh hymns are closely parallel, both in teaching and in style, with the poetry of Kabir as preserved in the *Bijak*, and with the hymns of the *Adi Granth* of the Sikhs. Thus, if a teacher of the line of Rai Das founded the Sadhs, the theology and ethics of the sect would be precisely what they are today, except for the Christian elements. Thus the statement given to Mr. Trant appears to be quite historical;[3] but it does not account for all the facts. Whence came the Christian elements?

'The Emperor Akbar had a house of worship erected at Fatehpur-Sikri in 1575; and thereafter he called a large number of Moslem religious teachers to the capital, and set them to discuss religious themes. But he soon tired of mere Moslem debates. He sent for Zoroastrians, Jains, and Hindus, and listened to them gladly; and also summoned Catholic priests from Goa. He finally lost all faith in Islam, and

[1] Among Ramananda's disciples were: Asanand, Kabir, Rai Dasi Pipa, Sursuranand, and others. Uday Das was a disciple of Rai Das, and Birbhan of Uday Das. The dates of the above are as follows: Ramananda *c.* A.D. 1430–70; Rai Das, *c.* 1470–1500; Uday Das, *c.* 1500–1530, Birbhan *c.* 1530–60. A.D. 1544 is the date of the origin of the Sadhs. (J.N.F.)

[2] See Trumpp, *The Sikh Granth*, pp. 130, 489–491, 666, 668. Account of Rai Das in *An Outline of Religious Literature* is erroneous. See p. 328, (J.N.F.)

[3] See above, pp. 30 ff.

founded a new religion of his own.[1] But, in spite of that, he remained most friendly with the Catholic Fathers, and allowed them to build churches and win converts. He issued a rescript against polygamy in A.D. 1587.

'His successors, Jehangir,[2] and Shah Jahan, were not quite so well-disposed to the Catholics; but even they did not drive the Fathers away; and from A.D. 1600 there was a succession of Jesuit priests in and around Agra and Delhi.

'Prince Dara Shikoh, the eldest son of Shah Jahan, was a man of religious and scholarly interests. He studied Hinduism, and had a group of the Upanishads translated into Persian. He was friendly with Baba Lal[3] a leader of the same type as Kabir, teaching strict monotheism and condemning idols. The Prince got court scribes to prepare an outline of Baba Lal's teaching in Persian. Both documents are extant. He had some of his great-grandfather's interests. Like him, he enjoyed intercourse with Christians. He was especially intimate with Father Busée, a Flemish Jesuit.[4]

'Jogi Das, who, according to Fisher, taught the Sadhs of the Delhi district, must have been a fighting ascetic; for, according to the information given to Fisher[5] by the Sadhs, he was one of the leaders of the Raja of Dholpur's army. Now the Raja unquestionably belonged to the party of Dara Shikoh; and, in all probability, he fought for the Prince against Aurengzeb in some of the battles of A.D. 1658. Aurengzeb proved victorious, and Dara Shikoh was put to death. All the leaders of the forces which had fought for Dara were thus in danger of their lives.[6]

'Hence, Jogi Das would flee in disguise. He would give up his fighting and become an inoffensive religious teacher, leading the simple life of a wandering ascetic. Since he was an ascetic, and belonged to Dara Shikoh's party, he was in all

[1] See Vincent Smith's *Akbar, the Great Mogul*.

[2] See Bernier's *Travels*, p. 289.

[3] See *Encyclopædia of Religion and Ethics*, s.v. Baba Lalis.

[4] See Vincent Smith's *Oxford History of India*, p. 409; Bernier's *Travels in the Moghul Empire*, pp. 7, 101, 244 and 289, (Oxford University Press) 1914.

[5] See above, pp. 19 ff.

[6] See Sarkar's statement above, p. 15.

probability one of the many religious men who were intimate with the Prince. If this guess is right, he would have abundance of opportunity of meeting Father Busée and other Christians.

'Since he taught the Sadhs of the Delhi district, it is a most plausible conjecture that to him the Sadhs owe their monogamy and the other Christian features of their teaching. These ideas, clearly, must have been brought to them by some one who had been under the influence of the Catholic Fathers. Christianity was altogether unknown in Northern India when Birbhan founded the sect in 1544. It is noteworthy that the date given by Fisher for Jogi Das is A.D. 1658. To Jogi Das, then, we attribute the Christian elements of the Sadh creed. He must have also written the *Adi Upadesa* which forbids polygamy. This piece of literature is also called "The Twelve Commandments," a phrase which is clearly modelled on "The Ten Commandments."[1] Thus the dual foundation of the sect is reflected in the two pieces of literature in which its faith is expressed.

'It is worthy of note that the *Adi Granth* of the Sikhs was compiled *c.* A.D. 1600, probably a century after the foundation of the sect. Many of the hymns belong, doubtless, to A.D. 1500 rather than to 1600; but many pieces are of late origin. Yet the whole work is named the *Adi Granth* or "Original Book," the idea being, not that the book as it is had existed from the birth of the sect, but that it contained the ancient teaching, that it was not a piece of new theology. There were recent things in it, yet the whole was of one piece. Hence the name was a bid for confidence.

THE 'ADI UPADESA'

'It is probable that the phrase *Adi Upadesa*, "The Original Teaching," was suggested by the title of the Sikh *Adi*

[1] Present day Sadhs do not agree that their code is in the form of Twelve Commandments. This error (if error it be) can probably be traced to the carelessness of H. H. Wilson (or one of his assistants). Farrukhabad Sadhs assure the writer that in the copies of the *Adi Upadesa* in their possession, there is no such division. At the same time they admit that all the materials listed under the twelve heads are to be found in the *Adi Upadesa*.

Granth, that it arose in similar circumstances and was coined with a similar purpose. Jogi Das felt that, if his rich teaching was not to be forgotten, it must be clearly expressed in a literary document. The serious and reflective character of the writer's mind shows itself in his choice of prose instead of verse, which hitherto had been the almost exclusive vehicle of religious teaching in the Hindi tongue. He was doubtless quite conscious of the fresh elements which he had brought to the Sadh community, but he also felt that the new was not at variance with the old, that the whole made one garment.

'In conclusion, let it be noted that Trant got his information at Farrukhabad, where Birbhan taught;[1] while Fisher got his in the neighbourhood of Delhi, where a trustworthy tradition about Jogi Das still existed.'

Additional Note

The writer greatly values the above statement which was so carefully prepared by his former counsellor, Dr. Farquhar. This appreciation is diminished not a whit by the fact that Dr. Farquhar's summary contains the words 'guess' and 'conjecture.' At this point we shall do well to notice the list of those scholars who had previously written about the Sadhs.—

In 1816 William Trant wrote on the Farrukhabad Sadhs.
In 1818 Henry Fisher wrote on the Delhi Sadhs.
In 1832 H. H. Wilson wrote on the Sadhs in general.
In 1896 Sir William Crooke wrote on the Sadhs, especially the Farrukhabad community.

The reader will have noticed that Dr. Farquhar refers in his discussion to only two of the above, namely Trant and Fisher. His reasons for not depending on Wilson's monograph are these: (1) Wilson himself never met any Sadhs, but had to depend upon Trant and Fisher for his materials. (2) There are at least two mistakes in Wilson's account: first he refers to the *Missionary Intelligencer* instead of the *Missionary Intelligence* (the right name); secondly, he states that Trant gives the date A.D. 1658, whereas Trant actually gives 1544. (3) Although Wilson refers to 'original

[1] Birbhan doubtless went to Farrukhabad as a missionary, but most probably his original home was farther to the north-west.

authorities consulted on the present occasion' (p. 353)[1] this sentence must be accepted with reservations, because Wilson's book was published in India the very year he left for England, and subsequent to his departure. Hence it is clear that his thesis on the Sadhs was either written very hurriedly on the eve of his sailing, or he finally found himself obliged to entrust the work to some one who possessed neither the interest nor the ability of Wilson himself. We must conclude then, that in following only Trant and Fisher, Dr. Farquhar was showing his usual genius in matters historic.

The following points in Dr. Farquhar's paper however, seem to the writer to rest on insufficient proof:

1. That Jogi Das was a fighting ascetic.
2. That Birbhan was the founder of the Sadhs, rather than Jogi Das.
3. That the founder of the Sadh religion necessarily had had personal relations with the Jesuit Fathers in the royal court, in order to become sufficiently acquainted with the tenets of Christianity.
4. That the *Adi Upadesa* was the Sadhs' authoritative holy book from the very beginning of the sect.

The writer has already stated his position regarding these points, in Chapter II. A further word in regard to the literature is necessary here.

Is it not probable that the *Nirvana Gyan* may have been the first piece of Sadh literature? It contains practically no Christian elements, but is closely akin to the kind of literature that Kabir and his literary contemporaries produced. Moreover, it is written in verse. It is difficult to believe that in those days, a new religion with a fervour and enthusiasm such as are found among the Sadhs, could have been founded upon a code of laws written in ordinary prose. Dr. Farquhar would perhaps reply by saying that of course the first generation Sadhs had their *Bani*, their hymn book. Yes, they doubtless had some sort of hymn book; but it was probably very much the same as the hymn books of other sects of that period.

[1] Wilson's *Essays on the Religion of the Hindus*, Vol I.

It seems reasonable to conjecture that the sect was actually founded on the teachings of the *Nirvana Gyan*, while the *Adi Upadesa* was composed at a subsequent date, after the doctrines of Christianity had been given sufficient time to become widespread. All are agreed that Christianity got its start in this part of India through the work of the Jesuit Fathers, some of whom found favour with the Mogul emperors. But in any case—whether the present writer is correct in placing Jogi Das first and Birbhan later, or whether Dr. Farquhar's 'guess' is right, that Birbhan lived first—it would seem to be in conformity with the humble origin of the Sadhs to believe that whoever their founder was, he was probably not a man of such intellectual and social attainments as to have been invited into the Emperor's court. The facts seem to require that more time be allowed for Christian teaching to have passed indirectly from the Jesuit Fathers of the court to the 'untutored saint' of the village, who became the founder of the Sadh religion.

It will be noticed that neither of the above viewpoints regarding the relative dates for Jogi Das and Birbhan agrees with the Sadh tradition that these two were brothers. The subject of the Sadh scriptures will be further discussed in Chapter VI.

PART II

CHAPTER VI

THE SADH SCRIPTURES

THE reader will remember that so far, in the discussion of the Sadh literature, three literary works have been mentioned, namely, the *Adi Upadesa* (the Original Teaching), the *Bani* or songs, and their Bible the *Nirvana Gyan* (the Knowledge of Nirvana, or the Knowledge of Eternal Bliss). In the present chapter the discussion is to be confined to the last one, the *Nirvana Gyan*. This book is commonly called the *Pothi*, the Book. It has never been printed. All the copies in existence are hand-made. The language is Hindi or Hindustani. The village Sadhs have very few copies; but the Farrukhabad Sadhs claim that in their community can be found from one to two hundred copies. It is said that in the large Sadh group in Bijamau, Bareilly, every family has its own copy. It has already been stated that the book is carefully guarded. It is not supposed to be even seen by any non-Sadh. They literally 'guard the deposit.' Mr. Trant in his article stated that he had received a copy of their holy book. It is not known what has become of that book. Nor is it known surely what book it was. It most certainly was not the *Nirvana Gyan*. It may have been a copy of the *Adi Upadesa*, but since the *Adi Upadesa* is rather a large volume, it is more probable that the book that Mr. Trant carried with so much care and pride back to London, was their *Bani*, their little volume of songs.

THE 'NIRVANA GYAN'

After ten years of acquaintance and fellowship with the Sadhs, the writer was rewarded by having his first glimpse of this curious and meticulously guarded book. First of all, one individual promised to get permission to show the book. Having agreed to show it, they appointed a time. Because of the uniqueness of the event a large number of Sadhs were present to witness this epoch-making episode, which took place in Farrukhabad, in 1930. No promise was ever made to dictate anything from the book. The fact that any line was ever dictated at all came about as a result of further patience on the part of the writer, plus the gradual increase of confidence and courage and courtesy on the part of the Sadh friends. The first sight of the book did not provide the thrill of having discovered a gold mine, but rather the satisfaction of perseverance rewarded. So far as is known the Sadhs today have no regrets for having allowed an outsider to see their Bible.

The copy produced for display on the above mentioned occasion was carefully wrapped in a cloth bag, which in turn was enclosed in a tin box. The book is about 12mo size and nearly one inch thick. It has a paper cover over the binding. The margins showed signs of many thumb-prints.[1]

There are 247 pages in this book, sixteen lines of hand-written Hindi poetry on each page. It contains a total of 4,200 lines, most of which are couplets, while the others are quatrains. Its 33,000 words make a book about equal in length to the first two Gospels. The writer experienced two thrills on the same day. Not only was he allowed to see the real Sadh Scripture, but he also heard some of its messages. This second treat seemed too much to hope for and was not fully realized until the actual words of the book had been heard. Laxmi Narayan Sadh, recognized spiritual leader of the Farrukhabad congregation, was the reader. He spread a cloth over a reading desk, laid on it the open book, reverently folded his hands and read. Not only did he read but he allowed his words to be copied. This came about by the extraction method. He read here and there the answers which the book gave to certain specific questions. Without the question-and-answer method it is doubtful if the treasury would ever have been opened. It was noticed that this

[1] Personal copy of Laxmi Narayan Sadh, of Farrukhabad, U.P.

particular copy at least had an index which facilitated the locating of names. The book is held in high, not to say superstitious, reverence. Once during the several hours conference, the long-legged Westerner got cramp in his knees and ventured to stretch out one of his legs, and inadvertently put his foot within eighteen inches of the book. Immediately he was requested to withdraw his offending member! The passages given below were collected bit by bit at four different conferences, covering a period of about eight months. At those times when the Sadhs seemed to feel that the visitor was too inquisitive, or too anxious to hear a certain passage, the matter was temporarily dropped and other points were taken up until the atmosphere cleared. It was an experience that brought the writer closer mentally and spiritually to the people of India than anything he had known before.

Quotations from the 'Nirvana Gyan'[1]

1.

Only God knows a man's record.

'Who can tell when a man has earned death and punishment for his sins, so long as he mixes good deeds with his evil ones?' This sentence was quoted in answer to the question: 'If eating meat is such a great sin, why does God allow flesh-consumers to live, not to say, prosper?'

2.

Even though a man receives the result of his earnings,
Nevertheless his occupation is determined by [*divine*]
command.

The Sadhs hold the Hindu doctrine of many incarnations for each soul. Past actions determine future births and conditions of life. Good Sadhs are reborn Sadhs. The ideal day will come when all souls are incarnated in men, rather than in animals. A newly created spirit is always first

[1] Invaluable aid in the translation was given by Professor Badri Narayan, M.A., LL.B., teacher of Hindi in Victoria College, Gwalior.

incarnated in a human body. [This seems to reverse the process of evolution.] This second quotation is an effort to state that a good God's providential will modifies His law of *karma.*

3.

He [*God*] *collected* (shancha), *and determined the age,*
Incarnation after incarnation has ordered man to be [*his*] *devotee* (bhagat).

God has made man in His own image. He has made men to worship Him and to glorify His name. This idea is not so well expressed here as it is in many passages of the Hindu *bhakti* literature.

4.

Mira Bai, Prahlad, Lakshman . . . Yogi Das, Birbhan . . .
Pandji (32, 93, 142)[1]

These names are found in three places in the *Nirvana Gyan.* Mira Bai is historical, and lived about A.D. 1515 to 1545. Many supernatural tales about her life are to be found in Hindi literature. There is a story of Prahlad in one of the Puranas.[2] Lakshman is the younger brother of the famous Ram Chandar, the hero of the Ramayana. Jogi Das and Birbhan, as already explained are, according to Sadh tradition, brothers, the last of the incarnations of divinity. 'Pandji' is probably a corruption of 'Pandit Ji,' but it is supposed by Sadhs to be a proper name.

5.

They sent the cup of poison to Mira Bai;
She drank, knowing [*its contents*] (113)

This reference is to one of the fabulous tales about Mira Bai, whose life was believed to be such that even poison could not harm her body.

6.

Prahlad depended upon Truth for his support,
And thus he escaped from the fire. (57)

[1] The numbers refer to pages in the copy of Laxmi Narayan Sadh.
[2] See also Crooke's *Popular Religion and Folklore of Northern India,* 1894, p. 387.

This is the same character mentioned above. He saved a cat and her kittens from death. His father became angered and tried to burn his son, but found that Prahlad, like Mira Bai, possessed a charmed life and was proof against the 'fiery furnace.' We notice that the stories themselves are not related in the *Nirvana Gyan.* One has to be versed, even steeped, in Hindi literature in order to understand the classical references. Prahlad is not a historical personage.

7.

You, a Brahman, have eaten goat's meat,
The True Guru has not so ordered [*us to do*].
Mahadeo says: Listen to this,
He who eats meat will go to hell (dozakh). (32)
The Brahman, even though he studied the Vedas,
Yet he made the mistake of eating meat. (100)

A later quotation will tell us that the Sadh religion became known in the third era. It is popularly supposed to have been disclosed to the outside world in this fashion: At Ellora, a literate Brahman became worldly by eating goat's meat. At the time he first tasted meat he asked all his friends to partake with him. A number refused because they said the True Guru forbade such a thing. From that time onward it was known that they (the vegetarians) belonged to a separate sect, namely the Sadh sect.

8.

The rest of the world knows it not.
According to Uda Das, 'yog' is the whole truth. (58)

The translation of the first line of this couplet is uncertain. 'Yog' means religious devotion developed by certain physical and mental exercises. For the system and literature of the 'Yoga' see Farquhar's *Outline of the Religious Literature of India.* Some Hindi books on this esoteric subject have been found among the Sadhs.

9

If you wish to be respected, tell the truth;
O men! always repeat the word 'Truth.' (59)

This is the best known of all the couplets in the *Nirvana Gyan*. Men, women and children are familiar with these words. It contains not only the essence of our ninth commandment, but in addition carries the idea of a search for truth in the abstract. It is the very first precept taught to Sadh children.

10.

Except 'Allah' there is none other,
Why worship a Muslim saint?

The word 'Allah' (God) is found three times in the *Nirvana Gyan*. The second line may mean: 'Oh you Muslims! why do you worship saints?' If the latter is the correct translation, then it is clearly an interpolation, most probably from Kabir. It seems to be out of place in the Sadhs' holy book.

11.

The irrefutable reply [in any discussion] is 'Param-para';
It is wrong to argue unduly over any point, when
'Param-para' is the proper and ready answer. (183)

'Param-para' seems to mean: 'Tradition says so.' This difficult passage illustrates the Sadhs' dictum that no outsider can understand their sacred book. This may be compared with another bit of advice given in the Sadh *Adi Upadesa*, namely: 'When asked what your religion is, simply reply, "I am Sadh."'

12.

When Kabir was in Benares (Kasi),
His name was changed to Uda Das: (73)
On the East is Kasi (Benares); on the West, Khasli (Bijesar),
In Kasi is Kabir; here (in Khasli) Uda Das. (207)

Kabir's name occurs about fifty times in the *Nirvana Gyan*. Sadhs are inclined to claim that the name means God; or that it is a title for Uda Das. They are not willing to give the historical Kabir any credit for helping to found their religion. However, this passage is further illustration of the theory that Sadh literature is closely related to that produced by Kabir. There is a clue here regarding the place of residence of the author of these lines. When he says 'here' he means Bijesar near Delhi. The name Uda Das is found about one hundred and fifteen times in the *Nirvana Gyan.*

13.

By divine order the first house was built at Ellora,
Seeing it [*as a pattern*] *men began to erect* [*their own*]. (25)

Sadhs take much pride in asserting that their religion is from the very beginning of time. They are much interested in stories of creation and the beginning of things. Bhawani Das was anxious to get from Mr. Trant a copy of the Old Testament in order to read the story of the Creation.[1] Umrau Singh Sadh[2] has written at some length on this same subject. Ellora is a place in the Nizam's Dominions famous for its caves, which are believed by Sadhs to have been the very first houses ever built—God's own handiwork. Some Sadhs have visited Ellora.

14.

In the First Era were Sadhs; *Sadhs also in the Second*;
In the Third Era they became known;
In the Present Age full revelation was manifested. (204)
In the twenty-fourth year of Vikram Samvat
[*Birbhan*] *had his vision* (hukm). (138)

The Sadhs believe that their religious faith has existed from the beginning of time, because their Scriptures tell them so. The story related above, as to how the Brahman fell into the sin of eating meat is supposed to have occurred sometime in the third era. In the present age (*kalyug*) Jogi Das and Birbhan were incarnated. The second of the above passages (138) does not yield itself to intelligible rendering in English. It seems to be an effort to fix the date of the reception of the divine command as received by Birbhan. Birbhan's name is not used but the word 'Spotless One' (*Neh-kalankh*) is believed by present day Sadhs to be one of Birbhan's names or titles. One Sadh tried to convince the writer that the above chronological reference means 1726 *Samvat.*[3]

[1] See above, p. 32. [2] Bartholbasi. [3] i.e. A.D. 1668.

15.

Although God created Muhammad, yet
Muhammad did not experience the vision (didar). (167)

This quotation seems to harmonize with Sadh ideas. They do not look upon Muhammad as an incarnation, nor as occupying the position of the True Teacher.

16.

Birbhan sings: When I obtained a vision (darshan)
Of the True Teacher (Sat Guru),
Then I experienced salvation' (mauj-moksh) (78)

Birbhan in Sadh scripture seems to enjoy a higher position of honour and reverence than does Jogi Das. In the above quotation we find the curious combination of an Arabic and a Sanskrit word to express the idea of salvation or release. (*mauj-moksh*).

17.

Greed, attachment, egotism reject;
Amiability and forbearance cultivate in your heart. (78)

This is another very familiar admonition. It is frequently quoted in conversation, and used often by Sadh writers. This short passage is good Hindi.

18.

'*Praise be to Ram! he deserved a brother like Lakshman,*
[*But*] *this pair is but a mere shadow when compared with*
The pair I am about to describe.
Let every one hear the narrative of these two,
Born in the Fourth Era, they are—Jogi Das and Birbhan. (142)

This passage has six Hindi lines. Only four lines appear in this translation. The last couplet refuses to be translated into English. The first couplet is racing, rhyming, rhythmic Hindi. The second couplet is fairly good poetry, while the third couplet is very poor, both from the linguistic and poetical standpoints. The third couplet, however, contains the names of Birbhan and Uda Das (or Udha Das). It will be recalled that in Chapter I a list of the incarnations believed in by Sadhs is given. The eight names given there are four pairs of brothers (supposedly). The names of Ram and Lakshman come second in the list. Since Jogi and Birbhan were the fourth and final pair, it seems strange that the comparison is not made (in the above quotation) with the third pair. On the other hand, the names of the second pair, Ram and Lakshman, are much more widely known in popular Hinduism than the names of the third pair (Krishna and Balbhadar). The question naturally arises, Does the narrative follow, in the *Nirvana Gyan*? Apparently the narrative of Jogi Das and Birbhan does not follow. If it does, it was thought prudent by Farrukhabad Sadhs not to reveal it. The *Nirvana Gyan* is not a volume of stories.

19.

[*Since*] *the serpent killed Mahadeo,*
The house of Parvati has become desolate.
Parvati came to the True Teacher, [*saying*],
Calamity has befallen my house, it was an evil day
When Mahadeo was bitten by the snake.
O True Teacher (Sat Guru) *be merciful to me,*
And cure Mahadeo.
Three posts were placed on a stool,
Mahadeo became alive and arose, and she was satisfied.
Kabir says: *Find out the mystery of this.* (46)

The translator says that this passage is good Hindi poetry, good enough to be worthy of Kabir's pen. It contains only one word of non-Hindi derivation. The story is of course a very familiar bit of Hindu folklore. The concluding lines regarding the *chauki* (stool) seem to have originated with Kabir, or with some Sadh writer.

20.

That whatever he told should happen,
That no shadow should be cast from his figure,
That he should tell him his thoughts,
That he should be suspended between heaven and earth,
That he should bring the dead to life. (46)

This paragraph, already quoted in Chapter IV, purports to state the signs of recognition by which Birbhan should know Uda Das when he (Uda Das) reappeared. The writer does not have the Hindi version of this passage. Indeed, he was not allowed to see the Hindi script of any passage in the *Nirvana Gyan*; hence he found it difficult at times to depend on phonetics for a correct rendering into Roman. But since he, and he alone, had gained this confidence of the Sadhs, it was deemed wise not to call in an outsider as an interpreter. The passages are in the main correct. The Sadhs probably do not realize that their dictation totals so many lines.

In the above passages from the *Nirvana Gyan* (omitting the final one) there are two hundred and seventy-nine words, after eliminating fifty-seven unimportant particles. Out of these two hundred and seventy-nine, twenty-five (verbs and nouns) are of Persian and Arabic origin. Of the fifty-five common nouns in all the lines, fourteen are of Persian and Arabic derivation. A study of the above statistics points to the conclusion that the *Nirvana Gyan* was composed sometime after the language imported by the Muhammadan conquerors had modified the Hindi tongue into what is now commonly called Hindustani.

THIRTY-TWO LINES FROM THE 'NIRVANA GYAN'

In response to a request that a passage of some considerable length be dictated, they agreed that a longer passage might be read, but not dictated. With due reverence and ceremony the preliminaries were carried out, and in the presence of twenty or more Sadhs the pastor, Laxmi Narayan Sadh, with folded hands, read two whole pages, after having (upon request) opened the book at random. All listened silently and when any form of the name of the Creator was heard, the older members of the group saluted by touching their right hands to their foreheads. It was explained that everything was being carried out according to their usual practice. He not only read the two pages, but here and there threw in explanations. The substance of the contents of these thirty-two lines which were read might be summarised as follows:

Take the name of the Master: remember the True One, ever take his name; put no trust in any idols, never expect to gain any benefit by going in pilgrimages to bathing places. Speak the truth. Take only the name of Hari Das. Have reverence only for the name of Uda Das.

It was stated that this passage of two pages is a fair speciman of the contents of the whole *Nirvana Gyan.*

A Sadh once took the writer to his house, and behind closed doors, put a genuine copy of the *Nirvana Gyan* into his hands. The long-sought prize was in his hands; but he knew that to accept it would be to incur the animosity of the whole local Sadh community, so very reluctantly he returned the book with thanks. Nothing, however, would bring him more pleasure than to be presented with a copy of this book, if this were given him from the hands of the recognized leaders of the Sadhs.

CHAPTER VII

THE SADHS' MORAL CODE

THE Sadhs are noted for the excellency of their moral teaching and practices. Dr. H. H. Wilson was the first European student to succeed in procuring any data regarding the content of the Sadhs' written moral code. He grouped the laws under twelve heads. This was accepted by some other scholars as the orthodox arrangement, and to these same men the conclusion seemed fair that the list of twelve indicated an imitation of the Hebrew-Christian decalogue. But it now seems clear that the arrangement under twelve heads is really a summary statement, and not at all according to the original Hindi manuscript. No such term as 'The Twelve Commandments' is in common use among the Sadhs of today. But the expression *Batis Niyam* (The Thirty-two Laws) is in use, and seems to come to Sadh lips as readily as the term 'The Ten Commandments' comes to a Westerner's. However, since the writer has not succeeded in harmonizing these two lists completely, they will be given separately. The list which immediately follows was procured from a group of leading Farrukhabad Sadhs in 1930. In each case the precept is expressed in only one word, usually a substantive. Some are abstract nouns. This will be shown in the translation. In each case an effort will be made to interpret the meaning of the word in a command or prohibition as the case may be.

THE THIRTY-TWO LAWS—*Batis Niyam*

1. *Contented one*—do not covet.
2. *One slow of speech*—practice moderation in speech.
3. *The disillusioned one*—seek only reality.
4. *The homeless one*—be a wanderer.

5. *Chastity*—be not sensual.
6. *Fearlessness*—fear no one.
7. *One who is free from bondage*—be free.
8. *Nirvana*—seek release.
9. *The all-wise one*—study all sacred sciences.
10. *The virtuous one*—be virtuous.
11. *The sifter*—get the gist of things.
12. *One who sees in true perspective*—be impartial. .
13. *The pure one* (title of Shiv)—be pure.
14. *Sannyasi*—control your passions.
15. *Truth-seeker*—demand the truth.
16. *The delightful one*—be amiable.
17. *The self-reliant one*—do not beg nor seek favours.
18. *The pride-less one*—do not be proud.
19. *The dispassionate one*—seek only spiritual things.
20. *The un-tasting one*—do not be a glutton.
21. *Patience*—exercise patience.
22. *Strength, power*—be a Brahmacharya or Biragi.
23. *Chastity*—rahat (रहत).
24. *Harmony with God's universe*—ramat (रमत).
25. *Guilelessness*—be free from artifice.
26. *The balanced one*—always control your emotions.
27. *One free from libertines*—practice no lasciviousness.
28. *One free from suspicion*—entertain no suspicions.
29. *Remembrance*—remember God continuously.
30. *Inclination*—incline your heart towards God.
31. *Enraptured one*—be immersed in spiritual meditation.
32. *Profound meditation*—think only about God.

Nos. 23 and 24 seem to be Arabic words whose meaning is not clear. The Sadh members who dictated this list and discussed it with the writer were not very familiar with it. Not one of them has ever memorized the list. One or two thought they could look over the list and check any errors, while the others admitted that it is not well known to them. This list is not taken from the *Nirvana Gyan*, although they believe that all of the above words are to be found in their Bible. These thirty-two rules may be called instructions for those who aspire to a highly developed religious life, while 'The Twelve Commandments' (their essence) given by Wilson might be called 'The Shorter Catechism' or 'Manual of Popular Religion' for the ordinary layman. While the name *Batis Niyam* seems quite familiar to Sadhs, the contents do not seem to be nearly so well known as the contents of the shorter list.

The Twelve Commandments[1]

Mr. Wilson made his translation about 1830–32. In 1896, it was copied by Sir William Crooke. It also appears in a condensed form in Hastings' *Encylopædia of Religion and Ethics*.[2] Mr. Wilson's statements are shown by quotation marks; while the explanations which follow each commandment have been gathered from Hindi writings of several Farrukhabad Sadhs.

1. 'Acknowledge but one God, who made and can destroy you, to whom there is none superior, and to whom alone worship is due, not to earth, nor stone, nor metal, nor wood nor trees, nor any created thing. There is but one Lord and the word of the Lord. He who meditates on falsehoods, and practises falsehood, commits sin, and he who commits sin, falls into hell.'

The chief thing in the Sadh religion is to identify the Creator. To do this one must withdraw himself from the world for religious purposes. There is only one God. He is the true form. Worship him who is Creator, Protector and Destroyer. Parmeshwar, Ishwar, Ram Chandar, Lakshman, Krishna, Bhagwan, Brahma, Vishnu, Shiv, Mary, Jesus, Muhammad are doers of great deeds, but are not incarnations. Men and animals, by their propagation and care of their offspring, development of skill, etc., show that they belong to the same species. But the superiority of man lies in this, that he has power to acquire knowledge of his Creator and to pursue the true way of life. Just as the many departments of government are all under one head, the king, so all laws of nature are brought into harmony by one God, the Creator. He is Creator, Master, True Incarnation, True Knowledge, and Father. He is eternal, fathomless, boundless; he is *Sat Avagat*. He is true, pure and holy. He is from the beginning and cannot be destroyed. He supplies all our needs, he supports the poor, he forgives, he gives salvation.

2. 'Be modest and humble, set not your affections on the

[1] *The Religious Sects of the Hindus*, Vol. I, p. 354.
[2] *Encyclopædia of Religion and Ethics*, Vol. IX.

world, adhere faithfully to your creed, and avoid intercourse with all not of your faith; eat not of another's food.'

Love not the material world. The world is full of tribulation and suffering; in humility endure. There are five causes of pain: (*a*) Failure to obtain the true religion. (*b*) To be in need of the necessities of life. (*c*) To suffer from any physical disease. (*d*) The departure of the soul from the body. (*e*) The migration of a soul from a human into an animal.

3. 'Never lie nor speak ill at any time to, or of, anything, of earth or water, of trees or animals. Let the tongue be employed in the praise of God. Never steal—neither wealth, nor land, nor beasts, nor pasture; distinguish your own from another's property, and be content with what you possess. Never imagine evil. Let not your eyes rest on improper objects, neither men, nor women, nor dances, nor shows.'

Mankind belongs to the animal kingdom; hence speak evil of no living creature. Steal no land, wealth, animals, birds nor anything. Let no evil thought come into your heart. Do not scandalize others. Never speak a falsehood. To do any of the above is to cause trouble, and trouble is contrary to the Creator's will. He who inflicts pain is a trouble-maker. The following things cause trouble to others: Unkindness, impoliteness, vulgarity, assault, theft, borrowing, kidnapping, and adultery. To gamble, to betray a trust, to act the hypocrite are all improper. A man can harm only that person whose *karma* (fate) allows it. Sins are of three kinds: physical, mental and vocal. (*Tan*, *man*, *vachan*.)

4. 'Listen not to evil discourse, nor to anything but the praises of the Creator, nor to tales, nor gossip, nor calumny, nor music, nor singing, except hymns; but then the only musical accompaniment must be in the mind.'

Sing only the songs of saints. The materials for hymns are within your soul. Do not seek them from outside. Have no part in any entertainment where musical instruments are used. Without an understanding of the 'Word' (*Shabda*) one cannot be free from *Karma*. Once armed with the Word one is eager for life's contests. In order to avoid evil discourse, gossip, etc., listen to the voice of God and employ your mind in his worship. The Word (*Shabda*—sound, voice, word) is the voice of God.[1]

5. 'Never covet anything, either of body or wealth: take not of another. God is the Giver of all things, as your trust is in him so shall you receive.'

Whatever we have is a gift from God; he bestows gifts in proportion to our faith. At the beginning of each of the Four Ages, the Creator has given knowledge. His last purpose was fulfilled on Twenty-seventh *Phagun Samvat*, 1726 (February A.D. 1668[2]). He has made the soul; the five elements; the three qualities: goodness, passion and ignorance; the three firmaments: earth, heaven and hell; the seven oceans and the nine parts of the universe.[3] Who can fulfil man's hope except the eternal Creator? Trust the One who holds the wealth of the world. Any one of the following is a breach of

[1] Dr. Robert E. Speer, Secretary of the Presbyterian Mission, New York, while visiting in Farrukhabad, was surprised to hear a Sadh say: 'In the beginning was the Word and the Word was God.' It is not known whether he got it from his own teaching or from his lessons in the Mission High School.

Discussing the doctrine of the *Shabda*, Dr. Westcott gives the following explanation:

'A doctrine which might be so described is taught in many Hindu religious sects, but it is not easy to determine in each particular case either the origin or the character of its teaching. In Kabir three thoughts seem to underlie such teaching:

'(*a*) All thought is expressed in language.

'(*b*) Every letter of the alphabet has significance.

'(*c*) The plurality of letters and words now in use will appear as one when disillusionment shall have been overcome. The two-lettered Ram seems to Kabir the nearest approach to the unity of truth or the letter-less one' (*Kabir and the Kabir Panth*, p. 74.)

Dr. Nicol Macnicol, commenting on the *Bijak* writes, '*Shabda* is thus the mysterious utterance of speech that conveys knowledge of the unknown and makes wise unto salvation. It is especially associated with the name of God, the *Sat Nam* (True Name) which is recognized in later doctrine as so powerful. . . . The doctrine is called *Shabd-marga* (Way of Word) indicating its close relation with that of Kabir, in whose teachings it has so prominent a part.'—*Indian Theism*, pp. 140, 157.

[2] Reference not traced. The Satnami Rebellion occurred in 1672. To the Sadhs, A.D. 1726 means the date of the revelation to Jogi Das.

[3] These nine names are given in the *Ramayana*.

trust: to keep a fast, to perform idol or fire worship, to utter the *Gayatri mantra*,[1] to take or give alms, to obey the Vedas, to make any man your guru, to believe in the caste system, to respect a hypocrite. Three things please God: meditation, a life of poverty, and dependence on God for protection.

6. 'When asked what you are, declare yourself a Sadh, speak not of caste, engage not in controversy, hold firm your faith, put not your hope in men.'

A knowledge of one's religious duty, *dharma*, reveals the road to salvation. But it is difficult to know one's duty, for this man says that the Vedas are the true religion, while that man declares that we find all truth in the Puranas, a third pins his hopes on, the Quran, a fourth follows the Christian Gospel, and a fifth finds his enlightenment in Buddha. Because of these various faiths, some lose confidence in all religions. The only safe rule is to say at all times: 'I am a Sadh.' He who holds no caste distinctions may become a fellow-believer. By taking a vow three times before the assembly, a man may become a Sadh. The True Guru possesses the true form, he speaks the divine truth, he knows all things, present, past and future. He can expound all knowledge, he reads the hearts of all men, he controls life and death, he treats all men impartially, he is blameless. Without a knowledge of this Guru, no man can hope to attain salvation.

With reference to this reverence for the guru, the writer wishes here to recall the fact that the Sadh religion has borrowed much from Kabir, directly or indirectly, and also from the systems of other sects that sprang up in the central part of India, largely as a result of Kabir's reformation. 'Sadh' comes from the word 'Sadhu' (Sanskrit, 'Pure, Saint-like'). Sadhu is a very common word in India, but the word Sadh is little known. Those who have not heard of the Sadh sect often confuse 'Sadh,' with 'Sadhu' when they hear it. From Kabir's time onward, devotion to the guru became a predominating element in modern religious movements in Hinduism. In the Sadh system we find that conception

[1] A special verse found in the *Rig Veda*.

highly developed and (shall we say) spiritualized. The word 'guru' does not appear in this commandment, nor indeed in any of the twelve, according to Wilson's translation. But the last clause, 'put not your trust in men,' implies that the only true guru is God. Present-day Sadhs, while they follow their religious leaders, yet hold firmly to the tenet that the only true teacher is the Creator.

Dr. Macnicol gives the historical background of this idea:

> They had need of an oral teacher; and when God was conceived of as spiritual, and one remote and hard to find, the importance of the mediation and instruction of a wise spiritual leader will at once be evident. Kabir himself was, as was natural, the chief guru of his followers; and it is not surprising to find him, in consequence, elevated by them presently to the rank of creator of the universe who is in all and in whom all is contained. 'I am Sadhu,' he is made to say, 'and all Sadhus dwell in me.'[1]

Many conversations with Sadhs led the writer to believe that the word 'Kabir,' in the mind of Sadhs, contains more of a divine or spiritual content of meaning, than of historical.

7. 'Wear white garments, use no pigments, nor collyrium [eye-salve], nor dentifrice, nor *menhdi* [red vegetable dye], nor mark your person, nor your forehead with sectarian distinctions, nor wear chaplets, nor rosaries, nor jewels.'

> *Sufed kapra pahinna, Bilkul Sadh ki rit rahna.*
> Wear white clothes, Live according to Sadh rules.

Do not wear red clothes. Do not use sandal, nor myrtle, nor *tilak*. Wear no garlands nor ornaments. To wear a sacred thread (*janeo*), to have long hair, to put on ashes, to wear bracelets, to go naked, to act dumb, to sit in a fire, to count a rosary—all such deeds are contrary to the Truth.

This seventh rule deals with such tangible things that it is rather easy for an observer to determine whether it is being obeyed. A local official once wrote 'that the order to wear plain clothes is more honoured in the breach than in the observance, the wealthy Sadhs of Farrukhabad being very gorgeous in their attire.'[2] Their clothes depend somewhat

[1] *Indian Theism*, p. 142. cf. Westcott, *Kabir and Kabir Panth*, p. 146.

[2] Mr. Steele, of Fatehgarh.

upon their purses. City Sadhs usually wear white clothes, while village women wear coloured clothes. They refrain from the use of pigments and similar bodily decorations. Jewellery is worn by those who can afford to buy it. The women wear a small tinsel ball (*bolla*) on top of their heads. They do not pierce their ears and noses. The Sadh men of Farrukhabad wear a small white stiff bowl-shaped hat. It looks like an American 'Derby,' with the rim knocked off, and is very becoming. The boys wear richly decorated caps. When a youth marries, he begins to wear a man's hat. No Sadhs have beards. Fine clothes and the special head-dress are modern sartorial developments. Village Sadhs wear the ordinary cloth head-dress (*pagri*). Some Sadhs use a rosary in prayer.

8. 'Never eat nor drink intoxicating substances, nor chew *pan*, nor smell perfumes, nor smoke tobacco, nor chew, nor smell opium, hold not up your hands, bow not down your head in the presence of idols, or of men.'

Do not partake of flesh, nor wine, nor drugs, nor betel-leaf, nor tobacco; people who indulge in these things are immoral, and are not following the true path (*sat-marga*). It is wrong to drink excreta; intoxicating drinks are excreta from the earth; hence it is wrong to drink them. Those who make use of any of these things weaken their mental powers and are unable to recognize the true faith. All Sadhs who infringe upon this rule are cast out of the brotherhood. One of our hymns says: 'Even give up milk in order to remember the name of the True Guru.' To worship any material thing or to do deference to any idol is superstition. It is better to give *ghi*, sweets, etc., to the hungry man than to waste them by devoting them to the Ganges.

In the *Imperial Gazetteer*, we read:

> The only caste peculiar to this district is that of the Sadhs, most of whom are cotton-printers by trade; they are distinguished by belonging to a special sect which does not recognize any idol worship nor the supremacy of the Brahmans.[1]

Here again we are reminded of 'Put not your hope in man.' Sadhs have developed a very distinctive manner of

[1] Vol. XII, p. 67.

salutation. They bow their heads to no one, not even to royal personages. They greet people by raising both hands, (or just one), palms outward, to the level of the chest. They may or may not express any word of vocal greeting. Among themselves they say *Sukh-Aram* (Happiness, Peace) and *Dandawat*, (Praise). The villagers use a modified form of this word thus, *Dandot.*

They engage in the service of no man. They think that to be the servant of any one other than God is to be irreligious. Each man has his own business, is his own master. Most of the city Sadhs are partners in small business companies. Few if any Sadhs are railway or government clerks or teachers. They willingly accept honorary service. During the great world war some village youths of Rohtak, Punjab, enlisted for military service. While this enlistment was looked upon as unorthodox, the boys upon their return were received back into the brotherhood. The writer saw a Sadh at the Magistrate's Durbar receive a certificate of merit for some altruistic service to his community.[1,2]

9. 'Take no life away, nor offer personal violence, nor give damnatory evidence, nor seize anything by force.'

The body of an animal is made for the dwelling place of a soul. To take life is to inflict pain. This is wrong, hence eating any kind of meat is wrong. Do not engage in the silk industry or in any other business which involves the death of small insects. Walk carefully so that no insect may be trampled under foot. Drink only filtered water. Buy only sound firewood, such as contains no worms. *Ahimsa* is God's first law. Always try to rescue small animals from death or injury.

10. 'Let a man wed one wife, and a woman one husband. Let not a man eat of a woman's leavings, but a woman may, of the man's, as may be the custom. Let the woman be obedient to the man.'

[1] In Fatehgarh, March 3, 1922.

[2] In Number VIII, we have evidence of Mr. Wilson's editing. This order contains two distinct ideas; temperance and prohibition of idol-worship. In the original there were probably no numbered paragraphs. Likewise Number IX contains two different ideas.

The writer has found that this tenth commandment is one of the most highly honoured and fully observed of the whole list. Sadhs do not marry twice in the same family. Men are permitted to re-marry, but widows are not. In 1922, one of their religious leaders, a man from Rohtak, Punjab, was asked to resign because he was not obeying the law of monogamy. Dr. J. N. Farquhar wrote, 'In their teaching, Christian influence is shown in at least one point, namely in the strict injunction of monogamy.'[1]

11. 'Assume not the garb of a mendicant, nor solicit alms, nor accept gifts. Have no dread of necromancy, neither have recourse to it. Know before you confide. The meetings of the pious are the only places of pilgrimage, but understand who are the pious before you salute them.'

Sadhs do not go on pilgrimages, do not consider the water of any river holy, offer no sweets, flowers or camphor to the Ganges.[2] They convince themselves that a man is worthy before they associate with him. In the midst of a group of true worshippers is to be found the embodiment of all rites, all pilgrimages and all piety.

The writer has discovered that the prohibition regarding alms has had to be modified. There are of course a few poor people among the Sadhs. They are not allowed to solicit alms from non-Sadhs; but they are taken care of by a poor fund, so that very rarely is it necessary for the poor to ask alms of any one. Sadhs are quite willing to accept gifts, such as photographs of themselves, and furthermore do not object to receiving free medical aid. No jugglers, nor magicians, nor dancing girls are allowed to assemble at their annual meetings.

12. 'Let not a Sadh be superstitious as to days, or to lunations, or to months or to the cries or appearances of birds or animals; let him seek only the will of the Lord.'

Have no faith in auspicious days, trust not in any one star, never consult a pandit about omens, entertain no fortune-tellers and wear no charms. Pay no heed to black cats, or to

[1] *Outline of the Religious Literature of India*, p. 344.
[2] Many Farrukhabad Sadhs keep Ganges water in their houses.

sneezing, or to ghosts. Call no Brahman for births, deaths or marriages.

The Charan Dasis, founded in the eighteenth century, may be compared with the Sadhs. Their system advocates a very exalted position for the guru, even to the point of identifying him with God. Their members are commanded

> not to lie, not to revile, not to speak harshly, not to discourse idly, not to steal, not to commit adultery, not to offer violence to any creature, not to imagine evil, not to cherish hatred and not to indulge in conceit or pride.[1]

H. H. Wilson, in his essay on the Kabir Panthis, gives the following summary:

> The Quaker-like spirit of the sect, their abhorrence of all violence, their regard for truth and the inobtrusiveness of their opinions, render them very inoffensive members of the state; their mendicants also never solicit alms, and in this capacity even they are less obnoxious than the many religious vagrants whom the rank soil of Hindu superstitions and the enervating operation of the Indian climate engender.[2]

It may be convenient in conclusion, to give a summary of Sadh rules.

1. Worship one God, the Creator and Master.
2. Follow your own creed; associate not with those of another faith.
3. Do not lie, steal, nor slander. Use your tongue to praise God.
4. Avoid all evil discourse; engage only in religious songs.
5. Do not covet; God is the All-giver.
6. Let your creed be: I am a Sadh.
7. Wear white clothes; eschew all adornments and marks.
8. Be temperate in all things; worship no idol.
9. Do not kill nor injure anything.
10. Observe monogamy.
11. Wear not a mendicant's clothes; ask no alms.
12. Be free from all superstitions as to days, omens, etc.

Probable Sources of Sadh Teachings

I. *Hindu elements*:

Caste, in regard to food and fellowship.
Ahimsa, non-violence and vegetarianism.

[1] N. Macnicol, '*Indian Theism*,' p. 157 seq.
[2] *Religious Sects of the Hindus*, Vol. I, p. 97.

Transmigration and *karma*, reverence for the cow, etc.
No strong drink, sins of *tan, man aur wachan.*

II. *Elements derived from Kabir and other reformers*:

One God→Creator, Master, *Avagat* and *Sat Guru.*
No leaders necessary in public worship.
No idolatry—obeisance to God alone.
Trust in God, the secret of peace of mind.
No pilgrimages nor mendicant's apparel.
No divine incarnations.
Prohibitions of covetousness (*Baba Lalis*), of theft, of lies, of adultery, of worldliness.
Importance of humility and patience.
Freedom from fear of omens, astrology, etc.

III. *Christian elements*:

Monogamy.
Sunday worship, or weekly worship.
The sacramental meal *Prasad.*

IV. *Elements of which the source is not clear*:

No evil thoughts, (*Charan Dasis?*) no idle talk, no hatred.
Avoid improper things, gossip, calumny, music, etc.
Take no alms, be no man's servant, seek only God's will.
Take no oath, do not go to law, give no damnatory evidence.
Never engage in controversy.
No sacred forms of worship, no sacred places.
Wearing white garments, temperance in all things, food, drink and clothing.

We may close this chapter with an account of a visit of the writer to the Farrukhabad Sadh ascetics. Sadhs who become sadhus do not continue this life of mendicancy for very long periods. One sadh remained a holy man for twelve years and then gave it up to engage in the ordinary pursuits of life. The sadhu visited, Anand Ram, is about thirty years of age.[1] His wife died several years ago, so he is alone. Sometimes he works in his brother's factory. Eight men were present on the occasion of this visit. The place was a roof-garden in a private park on the bank of the Ganges. The time was evening. Anand Ram was not accustomed to receiving outsiders as visitors. Dressed in his loin-cloth, he displayed no sectarian marks on his nearly naked body. His legs were

[1] In 1924, a year after this interview, he went on a pilgrimage to Hardwar, near the head-waters of the Ganges river.

crossed, not after the fashion of Buddha, but with one knee on top of the other, and one foot extended to either side. We all sat quiet for some minutes. In response to a question, he smiled, clasped his hands on the back of his head, and spoke clearly but not very fluently. He said God told him to become an ascetic. He makes no effort to win others to this manner of life. He spends some time in the city and occasionally speaks before the Sadh congregation. He eats once daily, about noon. His food is provided by his relatives. He sleeps three or four hours at a time. He rises for meditation about 3.0 a.m. Although he has been a Sadhu for five years, his muscles look solid and he seems to be sturdy. He is literate and is held in high esteem by his Sadh brothers. There was a marked contrast between this healthy clean man and the average decorated Hindu 'holy man' sitting in dust and dirt and ashes on the busiest corner of the city.

Jagphul Narayan is another Sadh sadhu. He stays in another garden near the Ganges, in Farrukhabad. The meeting with him was in the morning. While just as plain, and as nearly naked as Anand Ram, he was nevertheless different. He is young, inexperienced and naïve. Though more or less taken by surprise, he was quite unembarrassed. He gladly told what he knows of his religion. He is not a recluse. Sadhs gather at this place every evening. He occasionally does manual labour in the city. His father was present and the boy respectfully consulted him on several points. He had several Hindi books. He showed unusual interest in *From Passion to Peace*, a Hindi translation of which he was reading.[1] He has never spoken before the Sadh group. He recited the following lines, which he said he had learned from the *Gyan Sagar* (Ocean of Knowledge).[2]

> Four couplets there are—a quartet of pearls,
> Four things for your mind, to make you wise,
> O Brother give heed, turn your mind.
>
> Accept the True Name, from it never retreat,
> Remember it brother, at every heart-beat.

[1] By James Allen.

[2] He may have said *Gyan Sagar* by mistake. He probably meant the *Nirvana Gyan*, their holy book.

The second true pearl, O Sadh, will you heed,
Keep your tongue free from falsehood.
When tempted by lust, keep self above shame,
Your shelter, O Sadh! is in the True Name.
Keep silent unless to speak is your right;
Speak in your heart, day and night.

Sadhs resemble Hindus in that they have Hindi names, speak the Hindi language, wear a long lock of hair on the crown, dress more or less like Hindus (especially the rural people) and embrace much Hindu philosophy. They resemble Muslims in that they believe in the unity of God, they abhor idolatry, disregard the Ganges and holy places, and some of them bury their dead.

CHAPTER VIII

MARRIAGE CUSTOMS AND SONGS

MARRIAGE plays a very important rôle in Indian social life. Centuries ago, during the period in which the great Hindi classics were being compiled, Indian daughters exercised the right to choose their husbands; but nowadays in practically every community of the land, the choice of a bride is made by the father on behalf of his son. Among the more primitive peoples marriage customs are not only rather diversified but are also less mutable.

The Abbé Dubois found four ways of arranging marriages in India.

1. The bride's father bears all the expenses.
2. Parents of both parties share the expenses.
3. Poor parents sell their girls in marriage.
4. Very poor parents even give their girls away, to anyone who will arrange the marriage.[1]

Let us now consider the details of engagements and marriages among the Sadhs. Sir William Crooke has provided the most complete exposition of these ceremonies:

Children are betrothed in infancy, and marriage is solemnized from twelve to sixteen years. No bride-price is given, but the bride usually receives a dowry. As they all live close together [he refers to Farrukhabad] their betrothals are arranged privately among themselves. When the father of a youth contemplates his marriage with a certain girl, he sends a man or woman of his family as an envoy to the father of the girl. As they have no horoscope there is none of the endless bother so common among Hindus, trying to choose a proper day. If the father of the girl agrees to the proposal, he feeds the envoy with sweets, or makes him drink some milk and gives him money. This settles the engagement (*mangni pakki*). When the pair reach puberty the marriage day is fixed. Notice of the appointed

[1] *Hindu Manners, Customs, etc.*, p. 214.

day is sent by the father of the girl and on receipt of the message the boy's father calls a meeting of the members of the sect to whom the approaching marriage is announced. The envoy is fed and given a present of a turban and a sheet. During all this time songs called *mangal* [rejoicing] are sung. From that day begins the usual anointing of the bride and groom. Every day the members of the sect assemble at the *chauki*, and the *mangal* is recited.[1] On the wedding day the father of the bride gives a feast to all Sadhs at noon.[2] In the evening the bridegroom, accompanied by his father and friends, goes to the house of the bride, where they are all seated on a white floor-cloth. Opposite them the pair are seated on two cushions. After sitting in this way for a short time, the garments of the bride and groom are knotted together, and both of them move four times[3] around the cushions while some member of the sect sings or reads *mangal* verses. This constitutes the whole of the marriage ceremony. The binding portion of the service is the revolutions around the cushions. All then depart to the home of the bridegroom and the bride stays here for a short time; she is then escorted home by her brother[4] and when it is so arranged, she comes to live permanently with her husband but there is no further ceremony like the Hindu *Guana*.[5]

H. N. Misra gives the following description:

The boy and girl sit face to face.[6] For some time they meditate on God with their eyes closed, during which time the bride and groom tie their clothes together, and move four times around the cushions. Then the eldest man stands and asks: 'Have you accepted Sadh so-and-so and his wife?' They answer that they have accepted them. The leader then says 'Brethren' and the group responds with the same word. The bride returns to her home and does not come to live with her busband for four or five years.[7]

Umrau Singh Sadh furnishes the following information:

Sadhs marry within their own caste, but a man does not marry within his own family. Not according to the wishes of the bride and groom, but according to the wishes of the parents, the wedding arrangements are made. At the time of the ceremony the boy grasps the forefinger of the girl's right hand and they move four times around the cushions. Then the bride's father gives a dowry of clothes

[1] During a period of from ten to fifteen days.

[2] In Farrukhabad the feast is given the day before the wedding.

[3] That is, both go around both cushions.

[4] In the evening of the same day. These details indicate that this is a city arrangement and not suitable to homes far apart.

[5] *Tribes and Castes of N.W. Provinces and Oudh*, 1896, Vol. IV p. 245.

[6] No, they face the *Mohrayat*. The girl is in 'pardah.'

[7] 'Sadh Satnami' in *Prabhu Magazine*, 1920.

and cooking vessels and money to the groom's father, after which the father sends the girl home with her new husband. Sadhs read the ceremony; no Brahman is called. Whatever they give to the daughter they give not as a donation but they give it from a sense of duty. Sadhs do not invite dancing-girls to weddings. No musical instruments are used, nor are obscene songs permitted to be sung.[1]

Sadh women dress the bride, all parties singing as they work and striking up a new song for each garment they put on. The wedding gifts are arranged for display to the guests. The wedding proper takes place at noon. The priest (*mohrayat*)[2] takes charge of the ceremony. Sometimes there are two or more priests present. Some priests give instructions to the bride and groom in a formal lecture. It is customary to give an opportunity for any guest to state his objections to the impending wedding. Because of their freedom from Brahminical domination, they claim that their weddings may take place at any time of year, or at any time of the month. However, the usual wedding-season is March and April. Many weddings occur at the time of the annual festival (*Bhandara*). The parties do not sign any marriage register. Sadhs of different communities intermarry. If the size of the community makes it possible, the wedding is arranged within the local group. They usually marry within the Sadh community, but among the village Sadhs it is not uncommon for them to take a girl of a Hindu Jat family. Wealthy city Sadhs very rarely marry village girls. The *Rohtak* (*Punjab*) *Gazetteer* states that:

> At weddings they sing a song of their own, and the contracting parties walk around the chair seven times; but a Brahman is present only if the wedding is with a non-Sadh.[3]

We may compare this with the 'four times around the cushion,' the practice among the city Sadhs. Sadhs sing almost constantly at their wedding parties; men and women sing alternately, or both groups sing simultaneously. The knotting of the clothes is a Hindu custom. Speaking of its general use, Frazer tells us that:

[1] Bartholbasi, from his unpublished manuscripts.

[2] मोररात probably a corruption of *Purohit*.

[3] *Punjab District Gazetteer*, Vol. III, 1910, p. 160, article by E. Joseph, I.C.S.

The magical effect of knots in trammelling and obstructing human activity was believed to be manifested at marriage not less than at birth. From the Middle Ages down to the eighteenth century it was commonly held in Europe that the consummation of marriage could be prevented by anyone who while the ceremony was taking place either locked a door or tied a knot in a cord and then threw the lock or the cord away.[1]

Marriage Cushions

Sadhs say that the cushions used at the wedding possess no sentimental value, and hence are not kept as wedding mementoes. Farrukhabad Sadhs frankly admit that there is need for reform in their custom of early engagements and marriages. Some engagements are arranged when the children are only a few months old. This is perhaps due to the ambition of the middle-class people to marry their children into the families of wealthy Sadhs.

Divorce is reprobated, but may take place. Sir William Crooke says:

> They divorce their wives only when they have committed some offence which renders them liable to excommunication from the sect.[2]

Divorce is arranged quietly among themselves. Seldom do they have recourse to the courts. Only the husband has the right to initiate divorce proceedings.

Below is given a *Brahmachari* or wedding hymn. The writer of it says:

> When the bride and groom are seated on the wedding cushions, all[3] Sadhs chant the Brahmachari. This ceremony was first written and recited by Kabir.

A Brahmachari[4]

The grandeur of the occasion makes the serpent tremble,
At his trembling the good Master appears;
From his throne of 'Bhakti,' he says, 'Be my slave.'
(Glory and praise to Kabir the author of the ceremony.)

[1] *The Golden Bough*, one-vol. ed., p. 240.
[2] op. cit., p. 76-77. [3] Not 'all,' only two.
[4] Written (or copied) by Prithi Lal, ex-Sadh of Farrukhabad. See Appendix.

1. On an auspicious day in Sat Yug, a marriage was performed;
From the zenith to the depths of the sea, all were attentive.
The bride was Parvati, the bridegroom Mahadeo the Great,
From neither family was a dowry given.

2. On an auspicious day in Dwapar Yug, a marriage was celebrated;
From the seashore to the Ganges, all were attentive;
Sita was the bride, the great hero Ram Chandar the bridegroom,
The dowry was that of gold.

3. On a special day in Treta Yug, a marriage was celebrated;
From the Ganges to the Jumna, the wedding party extended;
Draupadi was the bride, the bridegroom Yudhisthir,
The dowry was given in silver.

4. On a special day in Kal Yug, a marriage was celebrated;
From the Jumna to the well, the bridal path extended,
The bride was Jaimanti, the bridegroom Raja Bhoj,
Surya was the pandit and rishis performed the ceremony,
The dowry was given in copper.[1]

Sadhs who have been consulted admit that the above translation is essentially correct; in any case, they do not choose to make further corrections. By comparing it with the list of incarnations honoured by the Sadhs (see page 6) it is seen that all the names are correct, with the possible exception of Raja Bhoj in the fourth stanza.

Another hymn, given below, is the best known marriage song among the Sadhs. The lines are fairly good Hindi poetry, the style is much better than that of the lines quoted from the *Nirvana Gyan*.

A Marriage Song

O Beloved Teacher, reveal thyself to me; without thee I suffer pain,
My soul is restless without thee; night and day I eat not, nor sleep,
Even at home my heart grieves because of separation from thee;
The dawning day brings no relief to my anxious spirit.

As falling rain, my eyes shed tears; I long for thee day and night,
Like a fish out of water does my whole being agonize for thee.
My breath is the wind, and on it is riding my heart to find thee;
I see thee in the night, my voice constantly utters thy praise.

[1] The persons named in this poem were the parents of Jogi Das and Birbhan, the founders of the Sadh religion. These four weddings evidently correspond to their idea of four pairs of incarnations, one pair in each age. See p. 6.

My good thoughts are my sword; knowledge of thee, O Guru, is my shield;
Remembrance is my arrow; meditation on thee is my bow.
Listen, Brother! hear the exhortations of the great sages;
They remind us that youth is always followed by old age.

Weeping, I knock at thy door; open it and reveal thyself;
O Lord, O Master! make no delay in revealing thy presence.
My fervent anxious heart overflows; how can I endure without thee?
Come to me, have mercy upon me, an unworthy sinner.

Remember my daily faults no longer against me;
O Great Deliverer of the soul, from sin redeem my honour.
Continually have mercy on me and forsake me not for a moment;
Cast thine eyes full on me and sever not thy love from me.[1]

Hindi of the Above

Darshan de guru! param sanehi! Tum bina dukh pāwai mori dehīn!

Niend na āwe ann na bhāwai; Bār bār mohīn birah satāwai;
Ghar angana mohīn kachhu na suhāe; Fajar bhai par birah ne jāe.
Nainan chhūtai salhal dhāra; Nis din panth nihārun tumhāra.
Jāise mīn marai binu nīra, Aise tum bina dukhat sharīra.

Dukhat tum bina; rotat duāre; pargat darshan dījiye;
Binti karūn mere sāniya bali jāun, bilam na kījiye!

Bibid bibid kar bhāyaun byākul bina dekhen chit na rahāi,
Tapat juāla uthat tan men, kathin dukh mero ko sahāi

Augun aprādhi dāya ki jai angun kachhu na bichāriyo,
Patil pānwan rakhu tati ab pal chhin na bisāriyo.
Dāya kījo, daras dījo, ab ki badi ko chhoriyo;
Bhar bhar nayanan nīrkhi dekhon nij saneh na totiyo.

Farrukhabad Sadhs acknowledge the above to be a fairly accurate rendering. Not only is this a hymn of the devotee to his maker, but it also expresses the intense devotion of the bride to her husband and acknowledged master.[2]

Sometimes a local poet composes a special song for his son's or his neighbour's nuptials. Weddings among the Sadhs are free from anything salacious, and are made very joyous occasions.

[1] Both the Hindi and English are given in Crooke's account.
[2] At the same time, they claim that all devotion is to God.

CHAPTER IX

DOMESTIC CUSTOMS, ANNUAL FESTIVALS, AND OCCUPATIONS

I. At Birth

The Sadhs claim to be free from superstitions and primitive customs pertaining to the birth of children. They believe that to marry and rear children is a fundamental part of normal life. But they are not free from the tradition that boy-babies are more welcome than girl-babies. They call no Brahman when a child is born. The child is named very soon after its birth; if possible by the grandfather, but if he is not alive, then the father or some other member decides what the name shall be. The choice of names follows the usual Oriental custom of religion and family tradition. No attention is paid to the day or the date of the birth, and no day is considered more lucky than another. When a poor man becomes a father, he distributes sweets to all his relatives; while the rich father is expected to give a feast to all his Sadh neighbours. On the eighth day after the birth, the mother is bathed, and is then looked upon as clean. It is reported from Mirzapur that the head of a Sadh child is shaved during the first year of its life. After the mother's ablutions the neighbours assemble at the home of the new child, and sweets, food or presents are given to friends and relatives.

The idea of *ahimsa* is ever present. One day two Sadh women took a sick child to the mission hospital at Fatehgarh. The doctor in treating the child removed an insect from its body and killed it. This act greatly displeased the women who had brought the child. Later on the child died; whereupon the doctor was informed that God had taken the child because He was angry on account of the doctor's cruel deed.

II. At Death

The background and atmosphere of death among the Hindus is vividly suggested in a passage from Crooke's well-known book:

> After the cremation the officiating Brahman touches fire and bathes, in order to purify himself and bar the return of the ghost; the relative who lights the funeral pyre keeps a piece of iron with him and goes about with a brass drinking vessel in his hand as a preservative against evil spirits while the period of mourning lasts.[1]

Sadhs are not indifferent to the inevitable 'Crossing the Bar.' Although their idea of death is that of the soul's passing from residence in one body to take up its abode in another, still the concept of death is not long forgotten. Even on feast days they remind themselves that some time their present existence must terminate. They spend most lavishly at the time of the annual *Bhandara*, and on similar occasions. They say they brought nothing into this world and can take nothing out of it; hence, eat, drink and be merry for tomorrow you may die. They believe they can acquire merit for the soul by this generous hospitality for the pleasure and benefit of their fellowmen. The following lines contain the essence of the Sadhs' thoughts about death:

> O foolish man, life is fast passing away, days are fleeting,
> Father, mother and children are all mortal.
> Even though my body becomes frail, my mind will entertain no doubts.
> When the final order comes, O Brother, rejoice in that day.
> All life is a dream, hence do not be proud.[2]

The following exposition of death customs is given by Umrau Singh Sadh of Farrukhabad:

> Sadhs do not inquire from Brahmans the time of death. They sing songs as they bear away their dead. They bury the corpse, or cremate it, or immerse it in a river. They do not tie *pan* to the body or do any kind of worship (*puja*). They do not observe the tenth and thirteenth days as the Hindus do; nor the third and fortieth days as the Muslims do. Most Sadhs consider such customs wrong. They hold it to be very praiseworthy not to weep nor to do any act of

[1] *Popular Religion and Folklore of Northern India*, p. 221.
[2] Sadh Sumachar, Farrukhabad.

mourning at the time of a funeral. Two or three days after the death, the bereaved ones give a feast and resume their business.[1]

At the moment of death it is not their custom to place the person outside on the ground as many Hindus do. If a priest or pious man is present, he prays at the time of the spirit's departure. The corpse is wrapped in a white cloth, is tied to a ladder-like frame and is borne away. Most Farrukhabad Sadhs consign their dead to the waters of the Ganges. Only men make up the funeral procession accompanying the bearers of the corpse; some go in advance singing. They usually bury at night. Four clay vessels are tied to the corners of the bier to make it sink. Wading into the water as far as they can, the carriers release the bier. Most rural Sadhs dispose of their dead at the burning ghat; but a few of them practise burial. There is a Sadh burial-ground near Farrukhabad. They inter in ordinary streams, too, for they look upon all waters alike as secular.

The injunction to refrain from mourning is observed by nearly all Sadhs. They say that God has given, and when He removes His gift what right has any one to offer objections by going into mourning. It is recorded in the *Rohtak* (Punjab) *Gazetteer* that the Sadh dead are disposed of either by burning or by throwing into streams; further we read:

> They used to dispose of their dead by setting the corpse against some tree in the jungle and leaving it to be devoured by wild animals.[2]

In this connection, Mr. C. D. Steele, formerly of Fatehgarh, writing to Sir William Crooke, stated that:

> A story is told (perhaps by their enemies) that in Nawabi [Muslim rulers] times, the funeral ceremony consisted in tying the corpse in a standing position to the tree with its face to the wind, and leaving it so. The practice is said to have been interdicted because of remonstrances of English officers.[2]

Present-day Sadhs admit the probability of such a custom in former times. Of the three methods of disposal, immersion, burning and burial, the last mentioned is the least practised. Their doctrine of death includes the belief in

[1] Unpublished writings of U. S. S. Bartholbasi.
[2] Crooke, op. cit. pp. 76–77.

many births, final release, and punishment for sinners. They do not seem to practise any of the common rites of ministering to and appeasing departed spirits. The following is a funeral song from one of their books.

Why be concerned for others, think of your own future;
O sleeper, abandon all unreal things which are perversions.
Worldly things are all transitory, says the voice of Truth;
In this village-like body are found five lions.
Gird on the sword of the knowledge of the True Teacher; and then,
O Brother, the angel of death will possess no terrors for you.
Duration of life is for a moment, yes, just for the twinkling of an eye,
The present opportunity will never be yours again,
The ship of life has set sail, you can steer it safe to harbour.
All your fellow-passengers stand ready with their loins girded;
Embrace the opportunity for choice ere the time be gone.
Disregard the things of the world, concentrate on the True Name;
Thus will you close the labour of this world, and gain the True Name.[1]

Sadhs sing and chant after the usual Oriental style. An account of the customs of the Mirzapur Sadhs has been given to the present author by one who lived beside them for many years.[2] The details agree with those set forth above, and tend to show that the smaller colonies of Sadhs have not deviated from the Sadh path.

III. The Bhandara[3]

The one big annual celebration observed by the Sadhs is the annual *Bhandara.* The word is derived from the Sanskrit and means, 'stock,' 'store-house,' 'full store-house.' At this time the Sadhs meet for several days, enjoy the fellowship of the brotherhood, and satisfy the inner man with daily feasts. The word Bhandara carries about the same concrete meaning for a Sadh boy that the terms 'Thanksgiving' and 'Harvest Home' hold for a western boy. In the *Farrukhabad Gazetteer* we read:

[1] Crooke op. cit. pp. 76-77.
[2] Mr. Ghosal, of Bhopal State.
[3] Not mentioned by Wilson or Crooke; Fisher merely refers to it when he states that in 1818 the annual meeting was held in Fatehgarh.

Connection with the other colonies of Sadhs is maintained by annual gatherings of the sect, held in turn at its various centres.[1]

In recent years the Bhandara has usually been held in Farrukhabad; but in 1921 it was held in Saharanpur. Umrau Singh Sadh, above-quoted, writes:

Once a year in the month Phagun, February[2], on the twenty-seventh day, the *Bhandara* is held. It lasts four days or more. In this annual gathering, members of the sect from all parts of India meet and discuss religious and other topics. No contribution of money is accepted from any Sadh who has become slack in his religious interests.

The Bhandhara takes place simultaneously with the Hindu festival of *Holi*. This is because the date for each is determined by the moon. It is often prolonged from four to nine or ten days. The length of the festivities depends on the spirit of the assembly and the liberality of the donators. If a man wishes to bear the expense of another day's feast, he announces the good news and the celebration continues. Prithi Lal gives this brief summary:

'All Sadhs, men and women, assemble with one accord. The Bhandara was established by the order of Gorakhji the Good Guru. The name of the Sadh who is to give the feast is announced. The meeting begins on the second half of the moon in Phagun, on Sunday.'[3]

This date agrees with the one given above; but of course it does not always fall on a Sunday. The meeting opens on the Sunday nearest to the fixed date. Who 'Gorakhji' is is not known. The name has probably been mis-spelled or wrongly copied. Prithi Lal goes on to record a prayer, which he says is offered at the close of the Bhandara:

O Master, give rest, set aside sin. Kabir says, 'When will these blessings be secured for devout Sadhs?' Grant that pious Sadhs may never be separated from him who is pure and full of goodness, whose heart is like the sea. Drive dull care away. Let no cloud of sorrow interfere with good cheer today.

They meet for several hours during the middle of the day, enjoy their banquet, visit, have religious meetings and

[1] *Farrukhabad Gazetteer*, 1911, p. 74.
[2] Thirteenth of the second half of the moon in Phagun (February-March). [3] See Appendix.

pass resolutions relating to the welfare of their own community. The members are never all present at any one time. In 1923 the number of Sadhs who came from outside places to Farrukhabad was estimated at five hundred. In 1931, a hundred and sixty Sadhs came to Farrukhabad from Bareilly District alone to celebrate this annual festival. All worldly affairs are set aside during this festival season. The happy event is made more pleasant by the singing of songs.

IV. The Sacrament

Once during each annual Bhandara comes the more serious time when the common meal is observed. This sacrament is called *Prasad* (Sanskrit, 'purity,' 'serenity' or 'propitiatory offering to a god'). The offering in this case is composed of four or five ingredients mixed together, which the Sadhs offer to the True Guru, that is, to God. They then divide it among themselves and eat it. Those present are expected to take some of the offering home to the members of the family who are not able to attend. This ceremony of Prasad is supposed to take place on the opening day of the Bhandara. We may here mention three terms which are used in connection with the sacramental or common meal. (1) *Prasad* refers to the food partaken of by all. They are very careful that none of it is allowed to be thrown away. Water is poured on the plate and any remaining crumbs are consumed by drinking this water. (2) *Charhaha* is a term used to mean any or all of the ingredients of the Prasad. (3) *Hurf* is a term applied to a religious feast given in the name of God by any Sadh as a memorial feast.[1]

V. Special Feasts

In addition to the Bhandara feast, special feasts are given occasionally. For instance, when two old enemies have become reconciled they express their thanks publicly by giving a feast to the whole brotherhood. Another event of a different nature happened on this wise: A telegram announced the

[1] The details of this paragraph were furnished by the Sadhs of Chiri Village, Rohtak District, Punjab.

death of a Sadh youth who was studying in another city. Later it was learned that the news was a false report; the boy was sound and well. The happy father, calling his boy home, gave a two-day thanksgiving feast. The writer was invited for about half-an-hour to attend this celebration, which was held in Farrukhabad. A feature of all such feasts, including the regular Bhandara, is that the men prepare the food. Even a member of the city municipal board on such occasions may be seen doing the work of a subordinate. Although the Bhandara occurs in the Hindu season of Holi, among Sadhs we find none of the horse-play and wild antics and coarse actions which are so common among Hindus at this season, and are even considered by some to be essential to the proper celebration of the Holi festival.

Any cases of discipline of the members of the sect are dealt with at the annual gathering. The following breaches of Sadh rules, if proved, make a person liable to discipline or even excommunication: Eating meat, subordination to anyone other than God, performing any kind of idolatrous worship, theft, gambling, and drinking intoxicants.

VI. Sadh Occupations

We turn now to the occupations of the Sadhs. No discussion of any social group would be complete without some explanation of their means of livelihood. One of the fundamentals of the Hindu caste system is (or was) the division of labour. This custom or rule may be compared to the guilds of Europe in the Middle Ages. In collating caste rules, Dr. Farquhar gives as the fourth rule:

> There is in each caste one occupation which is regarded as fully legitimate. Among the lower grades the rule is usually very stringent, but among the higher castes there is a wider choice. Even among the highest there are definite limits to liberty; indeed the *Gita* says it is better to keep to the caste occupation and do bad work, than to adopt another and do good work.[1]

Incidentally the Sadhs observe this caste rule, but like high caste Hindus, they exercise much liberty in varying from it.

[1] *The Crown of Hinduism*, pp. 160-64.

(*a*) *Cloth Printing*

People who know the Sadhs in a popular way, or have merely heard of them, understand them to be cloth-printers, and many such people suppose that the whole group is engaged in this industry. In the *Farrukhabad Gazetteer* we read:

> There are also Sadhs who till the soil, but they are townsfolk pure and simple. The cloth-printing industry is entirely in their hands, and the richer members of the community are bankers and merchants while some are land-owners. The poorer are traders and artisans.[1]

With regard to their chief industry, that of cloth-printing, we learn from the *Gazetteer* further that:

> Farrukhabad and Kanauj are celebrated for cloth printing as applied to curtains, quilts, table-cloths and the like; but the industry is languishing in Kanauj. A European demand for the articles produced at Farrukhabad has recently sprung up.[1]

From the same source we gather some technical knowledge of the industry:

> The indigenous tinctorial industries may be classified as follows:
>
> (*a*) Dyeing and calico-printing.
> (*b*) Tie-dying.
> (*c*) Printing and waxing.
> (*d*) Tinsel-printing.
>
> Calico-printing with wooden blocks. So very different are the styles of calico-printing met with in India that a promiscuous assortment may be arranged with almost unerring certainty under the names of the towns where they are produced. In Bengal this art is practised in one town only, Hajipur, near Patna. In the United Provinces, Lucknow, Kanauj, Farrukhabad, Jahangirabad and Jafarganj have each well marked styles of their own, but collectively their most characteristic feature is produced of minute and elaborate designs on white or coloured field; these correspond very closely with prints of Europe. Fuller's earth, castor oil, bee's wax, and gum are often used as resistants. The fabric is dyed for the ground-colour very often by means of a brush and in separate bands or panels. The colours are dull lemon, yellow, green, brick-red and orange.[2]

The modern industry of cloth-printing had its inception among the Sadhs in 1875, in the city of Farrukhabad. The

[1] p. 74.
[2] *Imperial Gazetteer*, Vol. XII, 1908, pp. 69 ff.

present name of the original company is Messrs. Sham Lal and Jugal Kishore Sadhs. In the writer's possession is a card indicating that this firm received the highest award at the Columbian Exposition in Chicago in 1893. At that time a Sadh was invited to the United States, but his family refused to allow him to go. Today there are no less than thirty companies engaged in the printing of cloth. They have developed great efficiency in their work. H. N. Misra writes of them:

> In the U.P. Exhibition of 1911 at Allahabad, one of the displays most praised was that of the printed articles of Sumer Chand and Sham Lal. Their curtains were stamped with beautiful birds of various colours, open flowers, sacred mountains, and beautiful forests. They were awarded a gold medal at the Universal Exhibition of 1900. In the Calcutta Art Exhibition, Lord Minto gave them a medal and high praise. In the Coronation of 1903, the rooms of His Excellency the Viceroy were decorated with Sadh curtains.[1]

Some companies have export trade, but most of them depend on local consumption for the disposal of their output.

(b) *The Sadhs as Weavers*

For many generations the Sadhs were engaged in weaving, and made coarse cloth and blankets.

(c) *Cotton Printing*

We give here a brief account of the printing process. They do very little (if any) weaving nowadays. Some print on Indian cloth, but the exporters use only European cloth. First let us visit the artist who is working out his conventionalized designs of birds, animals, trees, religious symbols, etc., on paper, in colour. His designs, while possessing no special artistic quality, yet show mathematical accuracy. Next we visit the wood-carver who, with the paper pictures before him, slowly and laboriously chisels out the design on a block of hard wood. These blocks vary in size from two-by-four inches, to fifteen-by-twenty inches. In this same courtyard we notice a fire-place, a pair of scales, some vessels, strainers, etc., and we learn that here the work-

[1] *Prabha Magazine*, 1920.

men, following the recipe, mix and prepare the colours. Except the man who does the weighing, these men and boys are unskilled labourers. At another place, the tailor is busy cutting the cloth into curtains and other articles of specified size. One imperfection in the work of all Sadh printers is, that all of the larger patterns are made from two pieces of cloth.

Now we are in a large room where are seated, each at his own bench, several men and boys, or in the larger shops, as many as twenty. These are the actual cloth-stampers or printers. Each man has at his side pots of colours and a number of wooden block-patterns; and before him on a smooth surface, is the cloth, having received its outline in black. If he is printing a border he may use the same block for some minutes; but if he is creating a bird or an elephant he will have to pick up a different block each time he touches the cloth. Stamping is done only on one side of the textile. Most firms use 'fast' colours. This work is all piece (contract) work. A small boy does a very simple design and earns a few annas a day, while the mature artisan earns a fair wage.

Now we visit the pressing-room. Here we find, not machinery, hot irons, etc., but instead, two or three men are folding and pounding the curtains with a smooth club. This final step is necessary, especially for export trade. Needless to say, all work is done by hand, except what the tailor does. We can scarcely distinguish a factory from a house, until we go inside. The most modern touch is to be found in a few of the largest factories, where we find typewriters in the offices.

The above is a description of one of the larger shops. In the smaller ones, we find that one man may carry the work through three or four stages. There is no fixed scale of wages and no labour organization among these workmen. Most of them are non-Sadhs. The Sadhs are the managers of the business and do the selling, etc. They close their shops on full-moon days and any special days of worship.

What can be said about patents? There are hundreds of designs, the simpler ones being the property of anyone who wishes to use them. But many of the manufacturers have their own special patterns which are registered in Calcutta. On the chemical side, no registered formula is required because this part is very simple. But lawsuits for the exclusive use of certain designs and patterns are not unknown.

The Sadhs take pride in their occupation; they feel that they are supplying the public with a useful and well-made article. They welcome visitors and gladly show their factories to anyone, especially a prospective customer. These tradesmen provide a good illustration of village industries, and any one interested in this problem could not do better than to make a study of the Sadhs in this busy zone of activity.

(*d*) *Other Occupations*

At the present time one of the members of the Board of Industries of the United Provinces Government is a Sadh. In spite of the fact that some Sadhs advocate that no money should be put out at interest, there are in Farrukhabad about a dozen Sadh bankers, and there are also some in Mirzapur and Bombay. In these respects the Sadhs may be compared to the Jains. (It is estimated that half the mercantile business of India passes through the hands of Jains.) There are also six or eight shops along general lines, managed by Sadhs in the Farrukhabad bazaar.

A few Sadhs have large land holdings near Kanauj and Kaimganj, both places in Farrukhabad district. The village Sadhs in the Southern Punjab are farmers, that is, farmers in the sense that they own and cultivate their own fields. The largest houses in some of the villages are owned by Sadhs. If reference is made to their apparent state of opulence, they usually answer with a smile of contradiction. The Sadhs have advanced so far beyond the rules of Hinduism that here and there an individual Sadh may be found in almost any occupation; but always on an independent basis.

CHAPTER X

EDUCATION AND LITERARY EFFORTS

I. Education

Among the city Sadhs, the percentage of literacy is much higher than the average for the whole of India; indeed the Sadhs as a whole stand above the national average in literacy. They have no schools of their own, either secular or religious, although in a sense their *chauki* may be called a school of religion. The Farrukhabad Sadhs send their boys to Hindi private schools, or enrol them in the Government schools, or engage private tutors for them. It is said that some Sadhs have a fear of modern education, because of its possible baneful effects upon their religion. Several Sadh boys attend the Farrukhabad Christian High School. They usually drop out of school after finishing Middle or Matriculation, and go into business. The Sadhs of the rural communities have only a slight interest in higher education. So far as we know only one Sadh has ever completed a college course.[1]

Some who have studied the Sadhs have formed a very favourable estimate of them. Thus H. N. Misra, after studying the Sadh creed and code, concludes by saying that we should all profit by their good example. On the other hand Grierson says that the Sadhs 'have wandered far from the Vaishnava teaching of Ramananda.'[2] Without trying to answer these statements pro or con, the writer wishes to present here two or three miscellaneous considerations.

[1] Bhola Singh Sadh, B.A., LL.B., Rohtak, Punjab.
[2] *Encyclopædia of Religion and Ethics*, Vol. IX.

II. Taboos

Just to what extent Sadhs practice *taboo* or believe in it, is difficult to ascertain. They certainly are not free from taboo in the use of names. Few women of any sect in India ever pronounce their husband's name. Sadh women, too, follow this custom. Two words deserve special reference. One of the names which Sadhs use for God is *Ap*, the polite form of the personal pronoun meaning 'you'. The word is rarely used at all by them, but when used, it means God and no one else. People who are used to being addressed by this polite form sometimes wonder why they are not so addressed by Sadhs. This peculiarity may account for their having in times past been beaten by military officers. Likewise, instead of using the term *Sahib* they use *Janab* (sir). These usages conform to their idea of universal equality and mutual respect, in salutations and greetings.

Prasad is also a very special word. As already stated, it is the name of the food which they devote to the True Guru and afterwards use in the common sacramental meal. Sadhs claim never to pronounce this word. Prasad is a very common personal name among Hindus; but no Sadh bears this name. If a Sadh has occasion to refer to a Hindu, one of whose names is Prasad (usually the last name), he pronounces the first word of the name but not the word Prasad.

Reference has already been made to *Sat Avagat*, an appelation of God. This name too, is highly revered, and rarely, if ever, pronounced. It is, however, not a widely used and familiar term, in the sense that the other two words are.

III. Public Speakers among the Sadhs

A number of Sadhs have the gift of public speech. It was once the writer's privilege to hear a public address in the Sadhs' chauki in Farrukhabad. The above mentioned Anand Ram was speaking on this occasion. In his speech he referred three times to Ram and Sita, the renowned hero and heroine of the Ramayana, and frequently repeated the injunction *sach bolo* (tell the truth). Another well-known Sadh speaker is Umarau Singh Sadh, of Barthol.

IV. Sadh Writers

Umrau Singh Sadh is also a writer of some note. In one of his Hindi manuscripts (translated by the writer) he divides his material into three chapters, in which he sets forth, 'What salvation is, who made the world, how it is proved, what the Creator's name is, how we must show devotion to God, and how we may remember Him and His purpose.' The subject matter, however, does not always measure up to the loftiness of the theme. He reminds us that Sadhs meet regularly in fellowship, and all turn their minds to those meditations which in their mind are most worthy. Further, we read that salvation can be obtained only by devotion to the true *dharma.* This is the all-absorbing subject; the correct answer to this question solves all our problems. It cheers one along life's path and provides comfort in time of adversity. How to please the Creator should engage our very best efforts. If we please God, our most cherished hopes will be fulfilled. The kind Creator does everything to make man happy. The things of the *Nirvana Gyan* are written in dark sayings. Its couplets are the words of inspired hermits and sages. It tells man how to become sinless. The most popular name for the Sadh faith is *Sadh Satnāmi Mat* (The religion of the True Name, Sadh.)

From the same writings we glean the following list of questions, which are given under the caption, 'The true test of Satnami Sadhs is whether they can answer the following questions':

1. Why have so many religions sprung up?
2. Where, when and by whom was the first book made?
3. Who was the first man? Where and when was he created?
4. What was the name of the first king? Who created him?
5. Where was cloth first made?
6. Where was the first house built? [It still stands.]
7. Who were Mahadeo and Parvati? Who performed their marriage?
8. Who was the first fruit of the womb?
9. Who were Hanuman and Narsingh?
10. Who was the Creator of the universe?
11. How shall we remove idleness from the world and make all men willing to work?

These questions are not a part of the Sadh creed and hence it is not surprising to find that most Sadhs could not pass an examination on this short catechism. The composer of the list himself gave only vague answers to some of the questions. Be that as it may, these questions give evidence that the background of all Sadh thinking is predominatingly Hindu philosophy. As regards the making of the first book, Sadhs claim that their book is older than the Vedas. Concerning the birth-place of the first man, the first king, and the location of the first house, we are referred to the well-known place of Ellora. The question about cloth need not surprise us, when we remember that many city Sadhs earn their living by cotton-printing, while their ancestors were weavers. Mahadeo and Parvati are looked upon as the 'Adam and Eve' of the race. The questions regarding Hanuman (the monkey-king) and Narsingh (the man-lion-incarnation) are based on Hindu mythology. The interrogation about the first-fruit of the womb involves some abstruse Oriental philosophy. In answer to the last question, we are told that idleness may be overcome by repeating the name of the Creator.

The following quotations from Sadh writings have reference to Christianity:

> By the power of devotion, Lakshman escaped from weapons, Parhalad escaped from the fire, Mira Bai escaped from the poison, but Mahatma Yisu (Jesus) did not escape from the cross.[1] . . . . Mary, Jesus and Mohammed were all ordinary people. . . . The Vedas, Puranas, Quran and the Gospel are words of men; the true secret of devotion came from the True Guru.

Otherwise the name of Jesus Christ does not appear in the Sadhs' holy book.

In these Sadh writings there is constant mention of transmigration and *ahimsa*; and nearly all the references are from Indian history and classical literature. The moral tone is high. The writers usually play the rôle of logician. Many illustrations are taken from everyday life, but the point of the illustration is not always clear. For instance, one Sadh writer argues thus:

[1] See Chap. vi.

Let us prove that there is one Creator for the whole world; just look at a river, how crooked it is, but a canal follows its own channel in a straight course as if conforming to a plan. Thus we know that the world has been made by One.

Below are given other quotations:

If poison is mixed with food, the crow, the monkey and the mongoose will not eat it.

As the real value of a diamond is known only in the hands of a jeweller, so we are rightly valued by the True Guru. [See Chap. vi. first quotation.]

A flesh wound may be cured by medicine, but the wound caused by harsh words remains forever in the heart of the offended.

A new truth strikes the heart like an arrow.

It is better to give food to the poor man than throw *ghi* and camphor into the holy fire.

Things made of the five elements can be felt when touched, but the True Guru cannot be so felt (sensed).

Everything is a part of the divine plan.

Ahimsa is the greatest *dharma*.

He who is steeped in religion is the embodiment of all holy places.[1]

In 1912, Umrau Singh Sadh, of Barthol, published a book entitled *Nasihat-ki-puriya* (Doses of advice).[2] It is of pocket-size, has one hundred and thirteen pages, and fourteen chapters. It is written in Hindi, with a sprinkling of English and Urdu. The style is simple, the printing is rather poor, and the circulation has been small. In it there is an effort towards scholarship, but many inaccurate statements are to be found. Much of the advice given is on a high level, but many of the arguments are not cogently stated. Below are given the titles and an epitome of the various chapters.

1. *Wisdom is priceless.* Get knowledge, teach your children. Piety and joy are products of education. Women too should become literate. Evil habits are not necessarily due to learning. Sita was both an educated woman and also an exemplary character.

2. *Effort, or perseverance.* Do not depend on your luck. Perseverance with the help of God will turn your luck from evil to good. Eschew laziness; never put off till tomorrow what should be done today.

3. *Courage.* Allah helps brave men. Shri Krishna was brave. Remember the story of the general and the ant.

[1] Compare *Batis Niyam*, found in Chap. vii.

[2] Revised edition, 1930.

4. *Thought, or meditation.* Always lay your plans before you begin a piece of work. Act in haste, repent at leisure. Girdhari Das is a good example of a careful man. The great progress of the Japanese has been due to their systematic thinking and methodical ways. A trained mind brings success and renown to any man.

5. *Rules of conduct.* Life is short; virtue is eternal. Therefore be regular in all personal habits. Go early to bed. Do a kind deed every day. Observe one day every week for worship and religious activities.[1] Do not waste one moment.

6. *Patience.* Patience will drive away discouragement. Adversity is the test of patience. 'A mustard seed does not grow on the palm' (proverb). Without patience no man can remain a government servant. Harischandar came out victorious in his test of patience. The Creator is on the side of the patient man. Develop patience by associating with upright men.

7. *Friendship.* Make friends. Share your joys and sorrows with your friends. See the value of friendship as it exists between England and America. Friendship is a great advertisement for the merchant. Do not keep company with gamblers and wicked men. Nobody likes pride, even in a raja. Selfishness is the chief obstacle to friendship.

8. *The spirit of forgiveness.* Develop a forgiving spirit. Return good for evil. Avoid court cases. Be slow to anger. Never engage in family quarrels. Do not pack anger around on your shoulders, [Cf. our phrase, 'chip on your shoulder'].

9. *Theft.* The Vedas, Puranas, Quran and Gospels all forbid theft. Be honest in business, for honesty is the best policy. Fear of robbery is a great hindrance to commerce.

10. *Falsehood.* Cultivate the habit of speaking the truth. Dasrath [in the *Ramayana*] is a good example of a man of integrity. A liar is a coward. Lying is a sin. Take the English as a good example of veracity. India's pathetic state is due to the prevalence of falsehood.[2]

11. *Sexual intercourse.* Moderation is the rule. Many evils attend child-marriage. Avoid obscene things and suggestive songs. The beauty of the home is a pure wife. Avoid self-indulgence. Be a loyal wife or husband.

12. *Egotism.* Affluence is conducive to egotism. A proud man forgets that God made him from a single drop. Pride brings many falls. Remember the fate of the haughty Ravan [in the *Ramayana.*] Continual pride paves the way to hell.

13. *Useful maxims.* [This chapter is a catalogue of two hundred and seventy-two maxims and almanac sayings. There is much verbosity. It contains information on every subject from the nine kinds of worship to the proper method of alighting from a moving train. To review the chapter here would be simply to repeat many things already mentioned.]

[1] This idea is evidently derived from the Jewish-Christian custom of weekly worship.

[2] This was written before nationalism had become popular.

14. *Concluding remarks*. Napoleon Bonaparte is a good example of iron will. He said that the word 'impossible' was not in his dictionary.

Some Sadhs read only their holy book. Others read also the Hindi classics. It was interesting to find in the home of a Sadh in Chiri, Rohtak, Punjab, a Hindi manual of physical exercises, with directions for the systematic regulation of breathing and control of the thoughts, in other words *Yoga*.[1] The book is probably an heirloom. The owner of the book was much interested in the subject of Yoga.

The chapter may close with a quotation from Prithi Lal[2] on what seems to have been his favourite subject, namely the *Shabda*, the Word, the Divine Voice, the Call of God.

The True Guru has favoured me by bestowing on me fearless devotion;
Where there is no fear, all delusions are removed.
The True Guru has removed all doubts by giving me Shabda;
He has been pleased to give me the immortal herb, immortality.
He alone is the True Sadh who can realize Shabda.
After the first step toward God, then the light of Shabda shines,
O brave man, keep Shabda in mind; cherish it in your heart.

He who lies awake planning how to obey is dear to the True Guru;
O True Guru, thy Shabda has been milk to me, it has removed darkness.

He has taught us that a desire for Shabda is a necklace of good,
Salvation gained, death overcome, my mind is in exultation.

O Master, thy Shabda has stood the test of my heart,
My pilgrimages in search of truth were all quite fruitless;
Having gradually obtained the truth, the whole world is mine.
Uda Das, pupil of Gorakh Ji, gave me this instruction.
In full realization, Jar Jodhan sings, 'The Truth is the real support.'[3]
O Sadhs, I have received a revelation through the Shabda.

O soul, without realizing God (Brahm) fear cannot be eliminated,
Without understanding Shabda, the bonds of Karma cannot be loosed.

[1] *Hat-i-yog, Pradi Prika*, by Brima Nand, 1833. cf. the Yoga Upanishads. cf. also Farquhar, *Outline of Religious Literature of India*, pp. 59, 80, 94

[2] The Sadh who was converted to Christianity. See Appendix.

[3] Jar Jodhan is mentioned in the *Nirvana Gyan*.

The True Teacher, our Master, has revealed to us his secrets,
When all doubts and delusions had been removed, I found the truth;
Knowledge of Shabda fulfilled my desire by making me fearless.

When Shabda comes into our hearts, how can he remain unknown?
Physical fatigue, mental doubts, are wholly removed instantly.

Having been inspired by the True Teacher, we put on our armour,
Having put on the armour of Shabda, we became eager to fight;
Let all followers of Uda Das advance to the front line.'[1]

In the original Hindi, these lines are in poetry, most of them in rhyming couplets. They are sketchy and set forth no complete doctrine of the Shabda; but they supply evidence that, to hear the voice of God, to experience Shabda in one's heart, is the loftiest ambition to which any mortal can aspire. Sadhs also use the mystical syllable *Om*; indeed Prithi Lal's manuscript begins with that magical word. It seems reasonable to assume that what Om means to the Hindu mystic, Shabda means to the Sadh.

[1] Is this a reference to Jogi Das, the 'fighting ascetic'?

CHAPTER XI

THE EVANGELIZATION OF THE SADHS

THE Sadh population is only a drop in the ocean of India's millions. But if we may interpret Jesus' saying regarding 'one of these little ones' as applying to the numerous little sects in India, we must conclude that we have as Christians a responsibility to discharge toward the Sadhs. Inasmuch as others from time to time have written abridged articles about the Satnami Sadhs, it has been considered worth while to make the present monograph as complete as possible. It must necessarily be rather comprehensive if it is to serve any evangelistic purpose.

Many Sadhs have expressed their appreciation of this work, and their desire to have an opportunity to read the completed paper. The writer feels and hopes that the acquaintances made and the friendships formed while collecting information will result in a step forward in mutual understanding and brotherhood—a step bringing us all one pace nearer to the fullness of the kingdom of our Lord and Saviour Jesus Christ. While it is true that, during these ten years of study, the writer has only occasionally been conscious of any explicit evangelistic intention, nevertheless the hope is cherished that this document will find its place among similar writings on other sects, and serve a useful purpose in bridging the chasm between Christianity and other Oriental religions.

The leaven of the Gospel has been at work in the Sadh communities. Efforts have been made by several to impart to the Sadhs the teachings of Christ. Mention has already been made of Mr. William Trant's visit to Farrukhabad, how he visited the local Sadhs there, secured a copy of one of their holy books, and had the privilege of explaining the content of (and giving a copy of) the Bible to one, Bhawani

Das. This event occurred in A.D. 1824. In 1870 the Farrukhabad Sadhs received honourable mention in missionary annals. The following is an extract from a history of the American Presbyterian Mission in India, prepared by the Rev. John Newton:

> Mrs. Kellogg found the work in the city of Farrukhabad continually growing in interest, and during this same year, reports six schools for girls and increasing opportunity for work in the zenanas. She received a peculiar welcome in the homes of the Sadhs, an interesting community of people. The Sadhs reject idolatry, caste and pantheism, but believe in transmigration and are careful of animal life and greatly rely on works of merit for salvation. Mr. Kellogg had felt much encouraged to labour among the Sadhs and had been invited to bring Mrs. Kellogg to talk with the women of the households.[1]

As a result of this and subsequent evangelistic efforts, about twenty years later (1890–92), two Sadhs, a young man and his aunt, were baptized. Their conversion offended the local Sadhs, and consequently resulted in the removal of the new converts to another station. Sadhs of the writer's acquaintance say that Prithi Lal became weak mentally before he was baptized. This rather disturbing event has now been largely forgotten. About that time, or a little later, the Farrukhabad Sadhs started on the road to financial success and economic independence. The present-day Sadhs are cordial and friendly, but do not seem to be hungering and thirsting after righteousness, at least not the righteousness that we know in the Gospel. Those Sadhs who do care for religious matters feel that they have themselves already found the true God and the path to peace.

More than a century ago, Chaplain Fisher observed that:

> The Sadhs have no regular order of priesthood. That man who in each particular division, happens to be considered most respectable, who can read, repeat their hymns and relate their traditions is their chief, though always with limited authority.[2]

This statement fairly well depicts the spiritual situation as it exists today in all Sadh communities. Fisher also mentions another fact which is also true to this day, namely that:

[1] Published in 1884. Report of 1870–71. The Rev. Dr. S. H. Kellogg, LL.D., author of *Grammar of the Hindi Language*, etc.

[2] op. cit., p. 24.

'Hindus generally seem to know very little about these people; and indeed to everybody to whom I have mentioned them, they appear quite a new object of interest and attention.'[1]

Th reason for this state of affairs is found to some extent in the Sadh creed. Theirs is an esoteric religion and hence not supposed to be spread through any public propaganda. Some light is thrown on the subject, too by the following statement: 'By caste I am Jat; by religion I am a Sadh.'[2]

There is no order of ascetics among the Sadhs. Even though one of their founders, Jogi Das, is reputed to have been a fighting ascetic, nevertheless the yellow robe and the cloister have been frowned upon by Sadhs. There are no Sadh priests with constituted authority, and they feel that to have priests is equivalent to obeying Brahmans. Sadhs have no endowments for religious purposes.

The Sadh faith has spread mainly by social contacts among the laymen. About 1915, a Jat of Khatkar, Jind State, because of intimacy with some Sadhs, embraced the Sadh religion. Today in that town there are several families of Sadh converts, most of whom are merchants. This example of conversion is unusual, rather than common. Three or four men of Rohtak District are well known locally as preachers whose influence has won converts to the Sadh faith. Commercial alliances and marriage arrangements play their part in the propagation of the Sadh religion. Schools and the Press are practically negligible influences in the Sadhs' methods of propaganda. Leadership along all lines is now largely in the hands of the Farrukhabad Sadhs.

Some extracts from Chaplain Fisher's letters will provide a more definite idea of the evangelistic service undertaken by him among the rural Sadhs. It has already been stated that Fisher's first impression was that he had discovered 'an extraordinary body of native Christians near Delhi.' But his first impression was given simply as a first impression—that is, he wrote to his friends after only a few months' acquaintance

[1] op. cit., p. 26.

[2] A common expression among the rural Sadhs. Farrukhabad Sadhs object to villagers' use of the name Jat.

with the Sadhs. In a letter to Mr. Thomason of Calcutta, we learn of 'a gathering of strangers from several villages to the west of Delhi in a *tope* (shrine, tower) near the Imperial City' (Delhi). They were found to be reading some books which had induced them to renounce caste, to intermarry in their own sect, and to lead a strict and holy life. Some five hundred people were present. Anand (the local preacher) found that the book which they were reading was 'the Gospel of our Lord, translated into the Hindustani tongue.' They were found to have many copies, some written, some printed. The people present claimed that this book was God's gift to them, and repudiated Anand's assertions that it was 'the book of the sahibs,' 'because the sahibs eat cow's flesh.'

They apparently got the copies of the Gospel from Hardwar, where a missionary (Chamberlain) had been distributing them; but because these people had never seen a *printed* book before, they supposed it had 'come from heaven.' The people were all dressed in white and could repeat the Lord's prayer individually.[1]

It seems likely that the above conditions were strictly local, perhaps confined to only one village. Doubtless the literate Sadhs of that time could distinguish their own book from another. One wonders, too, at the zeal that would cause these people to copy a whole Gospel, when they could be had so cheaply.

On page 204 of the volume of the *Missionary Register* already referred to, is another letter from Fisher to Thomason, which begins as follows; 'It appears that these poor strangers who have interested us so much are called Saadhs.' Reading on in the same letter, we are told that the Sadhs had existed as a distinct sect for fifty or sixty years; their chief centres were Farrukhabad and Mirzapore, but whether those groups had Christian Scriptures or not, was not known. Before the Delhi Sadhs obtained the Gospels, they had only 'a few written moral maxims and wise men's sayings.' 'The secession of Sadhs from Hinduism was not confined to one particular caste,' but they were all alike persecuted by

[1] See *The Missionary Register*, 1818, pp. 17–20. The letter above referred to is dated 6 May, 1817.

Brahmans. Their Gospels were in Henry Martyn's translation. They declined immediate baptism, saying: 'We will take bread and water and remember Christ, and we will sprinkle our brows, and vow to believe in Jesus.' The Sadhs have a great horror of beef-eating.

It seems from this description that Mr. Fisher never saw a copy of the Sadhs' holy book; in fact, apparently he never so much as heard that they had one. Of course the number of copies of the *Nirvana Gyan* must have been very limited in those days. Then, too, the lack of travel facilities kept the Sadh communities separated, and consequently their stock of common knowledge must have been meagre indeed. The phrase, 'sprinkle our brows,' given above, evidently refers to baptism. Did they really call themselves Christians, did they actually believe in baptism, that is, a sort of self-baptism? If they did, then they probably refused to be baptized by the foreigner, because he was an eater of flesh.

It has already been told how Fisher and his native helpers made a definite attempt at evangelization among these Sadhs, an effort which was maintained for several years, with the definite goal of baptism before them. One or two were eventually baptized. These relations with the missionaries, however, seem to have come to an end in 1827, after which date we read nothing more about 'these unusual Christians.'

It is quite possible that this particular group of Sadhs had no written copies of their own Scriptures. In fact, they may have been recent converts, or for some reason may not have known enough about their own faith to know that the Sadhs possessed a holy book of their own. Books, in the early part of the nineteenth century, were not commonly found in Indian rural homes. When Fisher states that they had only 'a few written maxims,' his statement is probably accurate as regards those particular Sadhs. The portion of their creed that they themselves would be able to recite was probably very slight. Fisher's apparent hurry to have them all baptized may have been due to his erroneous idea that they were so near to the Christian belief. Subsequently he must have modified his opinion on that point. Jai Singh's conversion seems never to have resulted in the real rooting of Christianity in that village.

It is a regrettable fact that of the evangelistic efforts put forth by Mr. Trant, Dr. and Mrs. Kellogg, Chaplain Fisher and others, none was continued long enough to prove a useful experiment. We dare to believe that if the 'witness' of any one of the above mentioned missionaries could have persisted for a period of twenty or twenty-five years, the leavening influence would have resulted in a goodly number of Sạdhs' embracing Christ as the fulfilment of their former faith. Indeed it may be that their original conversion to Sadhism was to some extent a matter of accommodation, rather than a, spiritual transaction. The movement began when multitudes were embracing the creed of Islam. The Sadh uprising whatever it was, must have taken the nature of a counter-reformation. It was a reform within Hinduism, and its complete break with Hinduism came only after the numbers were sufficiently large as to justify a separate sect. The new creed of the Sadhs was sufficiently like the creed of the Crescent to satisfy those people who had intentions of becoming Muhammadans; and yet the new doctrine retained enough of orthodox Hindu elements to save the adherents within the Hindu fold. In other words, the movement in its beginning provided the new converts with a psychological substitute for conversion, and as such, doubtless served to check the then rapidly-spreading Islam.

What do we find today in those villages where the Sadh religion was once a glowing belief and an active force? What conclusions may be drawn from the writer's diary, composed while visiting these villagers? If the reader will again refer to those details, he will see that the following points present themselves as evidence of the state of rural Sadhs today.[1]

1. The paucity of village Sadhs who attend the annual Bhandara. In spite of greatly improved facilities for travel, the number has greatly fallen off. This does not mean that the total number who are present at any one Bhandara is less (it may or may not be); but that the number of village Sadhs able to attend is much less, and the social and spiritual benefits accruing to any people from attendance upon this function, are greatly reduced in the case of rural Sadhs.

[1] See p. 16.

2. The fact that the Bhandara is now nearly always held in the city of Farrukhabad, whereas it used to occur nearly every year in one of the villages of Rohtak and neighbouring districts. This means one of two things: either it bespeaks an indifference to religious matters on the part of village Sadhs, or it is an indication of the overpowering influence of the wealth of city Sadhs. If the rural Sadhs had retained their religion in its state of former virility, this city move would have resulted, before this, in a schism; and the rural Sadhs would have established their own Bhandara. The fact that such an effort was made, and failed, indicates that rural Sadhs are becoming slack in their faith.

3. The tumble-down church in one of the villages which used to be the home of Sadh leaders makes one wonder what the condition of rural Sadhs would be today if there were no city communities of Sadhs. One can scarcely draw a parallel with the disappearance of the country churches in the West; for there good roads and the motor car are exerting an influence which so far is scarcely felt in rural India.

4. One whole village group has been excommunicated, because of laxity. Discipline, to be sure, is a sign of a thriving community; but in this case, the people themselves, as well as some of their Sadh neighbours, seemed to be uncertain as to whether they are 'in' or 'out.'

5. H. Sadh, an ex-soldier, has become a member of the Arya Samaj.

6. S. S. Sadh has become a sub-inspector of police. This shows that for him his religion is no longer an authority; for his religion forbids him to become a Government servant.

7. Sadh marriages among the Jats are rather common. This is probably not a new feature, and in some cases results in the increase of numbers, with a consequent deterioration of the Sadh belief. But this liberality in marriage is a position far removed from that described by Mr. Fisher, when he said that they would marry only within their own caste.

8. The scarcity of copies of the holy book in the homes of rural Sadhs does not necessarily mean that rural Sadhs have fewer copies than they once had; but it does mean that in proportion to the advance in education and in comparison

with the great number of Sadh Bibles found in city Sadh homes, the rural Sadhs are falling far behind.

9. The fact that rural Sadhs are no longer recorded as Sadhs in the Government census seems to indicate a laxity on the part of Sadhs as regards their religion. Their close relation to the Jats has brought about an identity with them, and apparently rural Sadhs have done nothing to prevent the obliteration of their name from the census rolls.

10. Bhola Singh Sadh of Rohtak adds this further reason, namely, that the modern age has debilitated the Sadh religion. Lack of substantial intellectual foundation has made it a prey to modern science and present day movements of thought.

Nevertheless, the present writer wishes to close on a more hopeful note. The Sadhs do have a helpful message for India. Having freed themselves from idolatry, they are a fitting example for millions of their brothers. The ignorance of Nature's laws, and the superstitious beliefs which are so prevalent in Hinduism, have largely been eradicated from their habits and customs.

By the exercise of an open mind and by their efforts to keep abreast of the times, the Sadhs have made considerable material progress. Their habits of industry, their ability to compete successfully in modern business, their taste for travel, their rule of total abstinence as regards the use of tobacco and liquors, their interest in world problems, and other good qualities have equipped the Sadhs for life in modern India.

As to their future, who can prophesy? Will the Sadh community grow or disappear? Will it be absorbed by the Arya Samaj, or the Theosophical Society, or will it be transformed by Christ's teaching? Unless their scattered colonies are drawn together by some fresh, strong bond of unity, the Sadhs will never have a centralized organization that can create a strong and enduring influence.

However, when the 'continuous increase in the momentum of the movement towards Christianity' has resulted in 'a new intellectual moral and social life,' the Satnami Sadhs will undoubtedly identify themselves with the new society. Dr. E. Stanley Jones once, while visiting the Farrukhabad

Sadhs, told one of the Sadh leaders that no possible harm could come from the present writer's investigations, and that he and his Sadh brothers should co-operate and give all the help they could in this study. The Sadh very quickly and politely agreed, but hurried on to the next subject, namely business—could Dr. Jones not give the names of several American merchants who would be willing to order Sadh products? So the question still stands: has the Sadh religion today enough spiritual vitality to hold a busy business man to spiritual values?

We close with a passage from the *Nirvana Gyan*, the book of books among the Sadhs:

> Early reflect on the greatness of the True Name;
> From His beneficence comes clothing,
> From His look, the gate of salvation.
> Nanak says: thus it is known,
> That He Himself is altogether truthful.[1]

We believe that some day, the One who is not only 'altogether truthful,' but also 'altogether lovely,' whose 'True Name' is 'the Name that is above every name,' will open before our Sadh brothers 'the gate of salvation.'

[1] Reference was not traced.

APPENDIX

THE following pages are a translation of a paper prepared by Prithi Lal, a Sadh who received Christian baptism in Farrukhabad, in the early nineties. After becoming a Christian, he voluntarily wrote what he knew of his former caste and religion. The manuscript came into the hands of the Rev. Dr. H. D. Griswold in 1894. In 1922, under Dr. Griswold's supervision, the pages were deciphered and copied by a pandit of Lahore. This fresh copy was kindly loaned to the writer.

The historical section is indefinite and perhaps also inaccurate. Whatever value it has lies chiefly in its poetical content and in the specimens of Sadh sayings and songs which were in popular usage among the Farrukhabad Sadhs at the close of the last century. They have changed little since that time. The copyist said that the spelling was poor and the grammar bad. It is the work of one who had had no training in writing. In several passages the meaning is ambiguous.

The translation was a slow and tedious task, relished least perhaps by an amateur. Four different pandits tried their prowess, patience and power on it! But we hope that the following pages may be useful, at least to those who already are well-versed in Hindi literature and folklore. The footnotes are the present writer's comments.

GENEALOGY OF UDA DAS, THE GURU OF THE SADHS

Two brothers, Uda Das and Gopal Das lived in the reign of Jahangir.[1] Gopal Das was five or six years older than his brother. When Uda Das was a young man he engaged in service on a trading ship belonging to Dalpat, a merchant. One time when this ship came near to a certain country, for

[1] A.D. 1605–27.

some cause it stopped and would not move. Upon this, the agents asked Uda Das to jump overboard, and relieve the distress. As soon as he jumped into the water, the ship was again on its way, and Uda Das was left behind. But what was his surprise to find himself on dry land instead of in the water![1] On that spot there was a temple, in which when Uda Das arrived an ascetic (*bairagi*) was walking. Seeing the holy man he advanced to the temple. When the holy man saw him he asked, 'Who are you and why have you come? and whither are you bound?' So Uda Das told the whole story of his adventure on Dalpat's vessel. Uda Das then said, 'I feel hungry.' His new friend gave him some sweets. Having eaten he remarked, 'I must find my way home.' Whereupon the hermit said, 'Sleep here on my bed, and when you awake you will find yourself in your own house.' Uda Das replied, 'I am unworthy to sleep on your bed.' 'Go and sleep,' was the command. He soon fell asleep and upon awakening he was in his accustomed bedroom. His family were all greatly surprised when Uda Das arose and presented himself next morning. They said, 'You went sailing on a merchantman; how have you returned?' Then he related the tale of his maritime experience.

Gopal Das had two sons whose names were Yogi Das and Birlal. They worshipped Saligram. One day Uda Das asked them, 'Whom are you worshipping?' They replied, 'Saligram.' Then Uda Das said further, 'Birlal, you yourself are Saligram, and Yogi Das you are Lakshman.' Birlal's wife was Shiamdevi, who said to her husband, 'This (Uda Das) is not my uncle-in-law but someone else.' Then Uda Das said, 'Shiamdevi, you are Sita.'[2]

About that time Uda Das began to go about preaching in villages to the north. He preached in Pulou, Kamli, Bijapur, Fatiabad, Manoherpur, Ajmere, and in the hill villages north of Delhi. He converted people into Sadhs and gave them his own mark as the insignia of the new sect. Some of his converts were Govardhan, Birlal, Yogidas, Lalman, Sundardas, Bhojraj, Brindabran, Haridas, Kahanji, Bhudhardas,

[1] This reminds us of Jonah.

[2] These are all Hindu names; it looks as if a change had been made to more respectable or higher caste names.

Khoja, Parusham, Pandaji, Shiamdas, Rupchandra, Govindgarib, Duryodhan and others. These converts all came into Delhi and along with them four women, namely, Shiamdevi, Basanti, Rajo and Goma. All Sadhs, men and women, stayed in the garden of the minister Rustam Khan, and there with great jubilation they sang their songs. Then Uda Das explained to his followers the customs of the temple. He gave new names to his converts, such as Ram, Lakshman, Mahadeo, and to the women, Gauri, Chandi, Sita, Dropati, etc. He made himself the master of ceremonies.

Their songs, sung in Delhi, are compiled under the name of *Nirvan Pothi.* These hymns were not all composed by Uda Das but are the work of many men and women. They are the fruit of the efforts of the above-named persons. They spent some time in Delhi developing their new system; every day the public heard their songs of praise.

Aurengzeb heard that a new sect had arisen in Delhi. When he heard that the Sadhs were celebrating in his minister's garden, he sent for the minister, saying, 'I hear that the folks staying at your house are establishing a new religious faith; now you must check them.' So the officer informed his friends of the royal decree. Uda Das spoke up, 'Who are you, Sir? We will kill the king, for he rules very wickedly.' The king at once ordered them to be killed before they could escape. So the royal troops were mustered out; the Sadhs made a stand and the battle was waged hotly. In the encounter five or ten Sadhs were killed and a few found safety in flight. Uda Das saw the Bairagi sitting on the king's elephant. He was the same man whom he had met on the sea-shore. When Uda Das gave the order to stop fighting, the guru hearing the command, ran and sat in the king's place. The others failing to hear the order went on fighting until all were killed, men and women. Uda Das fell, being pierced by an arrow from Aurengzeb's own hand. Mahadeo, a follower of Lalman was killed by the royal army on the field of Narnaul. The king's soldiers said to the few surviving Sadhs, 'Are you and your master the real Sadhs, descendants of Mahadeo, or are you just pretenders? Tell the truth about yourselves.' The foundation of the Sadhs' religion was laid by Uda Das in Delhi, during the reign of Aurengzeb.

The Sadhs' Book

Now hear something about Nirvana,[1] or the Sadhs' religion. The precepts of Uda Das which men must accept upon becoming Sadhs. The guru says to the new candidate, 'O child, why are you standing here?' He replies, 'I have come to get salvation' (*mukti*). Guru, 'Have you faith in my religion?' Pupil, 'I now accept your religion as the highest truth.' 'Among Hindus and Muhammadans, I wish to be called a speaker of the truth, a Satnam; Uda Das is my teacher (*Bawa*) and I am his disciple.' Then the initiate prostrates himself and salutes his guru (*Dandawat Salam*). This is the extent of the initiation. Usually the guru sings some song to his new disciple:

Disciple of Uda Das, go remember that Jogi who has performed all worship;
We meet Kabir Das, who gave some many benefits to his followers;
Now we know the first precepts of the Jogi.
A cup of poison was sent to Mira Bai[2] and she drank it knowingly:
Likewise believers have fully accepted the teachings of Gorakhji, pupil of Uda Das;
Ram Lal Das sings; the good Guru appears,
He who comes to feet of this good (true) Guru, really lives.

The Parsad

They spread a cloth before them, put some sweets on it and read some of the guru's teachings. The sweets offering is called Parsad.

Uda Das's Words about Nirvana

All Sadhs are dependent upon the first True Guru. Hindus say, Ram, Ram; It is better to say that God (*Khuda*) is One as the Muslims do. One who remembers heaven and earth is fearless. One who understands the teacher's message knows the secrets of the heart. The followers of Uda Das were the rightful claimants to his creed.

All Sadhs and sisters who heard these pious words were

[1] From Sanskrit, Nirvana, extinguished, final emancipation; the main word in Buddhism.

[2] A historical character.

enlightened. Each sang his own song. The songs are in a book, the *Pothi*. Except the truth in this book there is no other true knowledge of a redeemer (*moksha-data*). In the hymns the same ideas are expressed in different words. The wish of every Sadh is that the words which he sings be accepted by everyone as the truth.

Chand and Kukas founded a religion based on the Vedas.[1]

Kanji sings that he sees a true guru in the person of Uda Das. When Kanji sings, others are thrilled; they are mystified by his wonderful songs and the first words of Uda Das.

Sadhs offer to God *mawa* and *koa* (thick milk).

Before they recite their verses, they spread a white cloth, then place food, (*halwa* and *batasi*) on it. This is Parsad.

The Song of Ram Chandar

O Sadhs, the memorial of a good man is reality;
Put yourself at the feet of God (Onkar); earth and sky will be seen.
Ram Chandar, by Gorakh Ji, was made a disciple of Uda Das;
Ram Chandar sings—the True Guru appears;
When he sings, one's mind becomes ecstatic.

Third Song

O Sadhs! be happy by remembering a good man;
O Man! unless you see the form of the True Guru,
You will have to endure many births.
If you would understand fully the words of the True Guru,
You must turn your mind away from all earthly things.
If you wish to worship by making pilgrimages, and by fasts,
Do so without feeling ashamed before your fellow-men. Khan Ji sings;
By following Gorakh Ji, the *chela* of Uda Das, you will reach your goal;
A True Guru comes; seek his protection, and reach your destination.

Kabir's Writing about Offering to (God)[2]

After receiving back the offering made to God (Avagat),
The heart glows with inspiration; then concentrate (on God).
O Companion! it is our purpose to obtain the Inaccessible.
By drinking the foot-washing of a guru, a *chela* is freed from rebirths.[3]

[1] Most ancient collection of Hindu hymns.
[2] i.e. Parsad.
[3] This is certainly not modern Sadh doctrine.

Enlightenment brings full pleasure; in my ecstasy I fear not the Lord of Death (Yam);
He who walks according to my words is free from rebirths.

The Bhandara[1]

All Sadhs, men and women, meet with one accord in the assembly. The Bhandara was originated by the advice of Gorakh Ji, the noble guru. The name of the Sadh who is to give the Bhandara is announced. For example, it is given by S. S. Lal Sadh, on the thirteenth of second half of moon, in month Phagun, on Sunday or Monday. This is the customary arrangement. At the close of the Bhandara, the following prayer is offered by all;

Give rest, remove pain, set aside sins. Kabir say, 'When will these blessings be secured to devout Sadhs?' Grant that patient Sadhs may not be separated from Kabir, but that they may ever remain close to him who is pure, full of goodness, whose heart is like the sea.

Other Verses

Ascribe greatness to the faqirs of Uda Das.
Remove the dim flickering of the lamp;
Drive dull care away; let no cloud of sorrow interfere with good cheer today;
Help us to make no distinction between Hindus and Muslims.
In the twinkling of an eye the Good Guru has come.
In the great darkness of the Kaliyuga[2] this great *mela* (Bhandara) was established.
At that time the True Guru sifted the truth from other things.
Govind Garib says the above words are true.

Sadhs' Marriage Ceremony

In their tongue the Sadhs call the ceremony *Bramachari*.[3] The bride and bridegroom make four circles (around the centre). All Sadhs recite Bramachari and make offerings. This ceremony was written and first recited by Kabir, him whom the Sadhs call their master. Then in the presence of all, the clothes of bride and bridegroom are knotted together. They are seated on two cloth cushions. Then a poem called Bramachari is recited.

[1] Sanskrit—a store house, plenty.
[2] Fourth and last period of time according to Hindu cosmology.
[3] Divinity student, period of celibacy.

Bramachari

The impressiveness of the ceremony caused the Serpent to tremble;[1]
At the trembling of the Serpent, the Good Sahib (God) appears;
From his throne of bhakti, won by *karma*, he says, 'Become a servant.'

Praise is ascribed to Kabir who composed the Bramachari.

When the ceremony is finished, all together they sing four *Bani* (songs).

1. On an auspicious day in the Shrisat Yug a marriage was performed;
   From zenith to the bottom of the sea, all are interested;
   The bride is Parvati, the bridegroom, Mahadeo, the greatest of sages,
   From either side no dowry is given.

2. On an auspicious day in Dvapara Yuga, a marriage was performed;
   Sita was the bride, Ram Chandar the noble sage was the groom;
   From the sea to the Ganges, all were attentive to the ceremony,
   A golden dowry was given.

3. In the Treta Yuga a marriage was solemnized,
   Dropati was the bride, Udisthir was the bridegroom;
   From Ganges to Jumna, the wedding hall extened;
   The marriage fee was silver.

4. In Kali Yuga (age) a marriage was performed;
   Bhanmati was the bride, the groom was Raja Bhoj;
   From the Jumna to the well, the bridal path extended;
   Suriya (sun) was the pandit, and *rishis* conducted the ceremony:
   The dowry this time was copper.

The *Sakhochar*[2] is finished. It is used on all occasions. He who knows Sakhochar is a pandit.

Uda Das continued to preach in the villages. His converts sang their songs at his feet.

First Song

The songs of the feet prove to be the words of God (Bawa Ji);
They proved also to be the words of Uda Das.
By drinking, a dead child has come again to life;
By washing, Sahib has removed all our sins (kalank).
When I thought within me, then I got a vision of you.
O Kabir! you should give me that voice (Shabd) which God gave me;
O Sahib! remove the pain of which we sing in our poverty;
One who has bowed at the feet of Sahib is really alive.

[1] Hindu mythology. [2] *Sakhochar*—family history.

Second Song

In my mind I always remember the feet of Bawa Ji;
I do obeisance at the feet of Uda Das and his disciples.

(*The village women are singing, seated in the room*)
In this world we dwell in God's truth; we see him;
Because of delusion, we see him as if looking through thin paper;
You have made a wise decision on the religious quarrel between Hindus and Muslims;
Yes, Sahib, in Kasi (Benares) he was called Kabir; but here he goes by the name of Uda Das.
His servant humbly sings, asking that he may remain his disciple in all his incarnations.

Third Song

My mind is full of the thoughts of the feet of Bawa Ji.
I also meditate on the feet of Uda Das;
Yes, sir, Sahib, you existed before the word Onkar (Om);
Sahib is the guru; all others are learners (chele);
What a good religion you have started in earth and sky.
Sun and moon also show forth thy glory;
In thee, all delusion (*maya*) about Brahma, Vishnu and Mahesh is removed.
Ram who brought much hardship was called the son of Dashrat;
Krishna an incarnation, was born to Deo, and was nourished in the lap of Yashoda.
O Sahib, the world is ready to fill us, but we have brought nothing in our hands,
O Sahib, Gorakh Ji, pupil of Uda Das, gave the secret of fearlessness;
The Good Guru appeared, Birbhan and the Sadhs came singing to meet him, to be in his good company.

Fourth Song

Blessed are the feet of Bawa Ji; blessed the feet of Uda Das;
What a pleasure to touch their feet; all doubts are removed.
With the ardour of a devotee they sing fearlessly every moment.
The teachings of the Vedas, the Hindus and Muslims are different;
True Guru appears, the Sadhs sing to Govardhan (Krishna);
O Guru, he who seeks your shelter is in safety.

Fifth Song

Rejoice in the words of Bawa Ji; also in the words of Uda Das;
The world is full of delusion (bharam), it is difficult to see reality.
O Sahib, the stigma of delusion has been washed away by singing and companionship of Sadhs.
The words (shabd) of Gorakh, pupil of Uda Das, bring pleasure;
Yes Sahib, the true Guru has come; Sadhs sing with Kanji and derive everlasting happiness.

Sixth Song

O Uda Das, Sir, whatever you say suits your character;
O God (avagat), by your order there is an eternal body.
O Teacher, whatever you utter is most fitting;
In presence of the True Guru Sadhs sing in happy communion.

Seventh Song

Bawa Ji, whatever you say comes to pass;
Bawa Ji, he is fortunate who hears thy words (shabd);
Hearing words of Uda Das' disciple, darkness is removed from the heart as if by a lamp;
Knowledge is in my heart; my feet are on the true path;
Exultant in song, enlightened by your order, we walk on the true path.

Nirvana Bani

There is no wealth like Shabd, if a man knows how to utter them;
The essence is in the heart, Shabd cannot be purchased.
Shabd is coloured as by fire; it is more precious than pearls.
He who belies his own words, let his tongue be split,
He whose tongue is untrustworthy is not an amiable person;
In our songs we ascribe honour to the truthful man.

Who vacillates in speech, his pleasure is turned into pain,
For such a one earth and sky become a foreign dwelling place.
Earth and sky are corruptible; his word shall never pass away;
Life and death have their part, even the ocean may dry up,
But the testimony of a veracious man will stand for ever.

Trust, if substituted for, is no longer trust;
It can always be found in the heart of an honest person;
Without dependable words, fear will eat into your heart;
What an error to accept any substitute for veracity!
Teachers say that a truthful man is sufficient proof of this;
From the mouth of a veracious man, truth comes spontaneously.
No one ever feels pain because of an honest man's speech;
His words are as stable as a peg;
At no time does he feel inclined to utter unreliable speech.

The name of Uda Das is celebrated in song;
Rejoicing, festoons on doors, speak of the marriage in Ceylon:
The 'pardah' woman is chaste, the free woman, unchaste;
The bride of Ceylon is the true type.[1]
There is only one thing really hidden, the secret of true religion.

[1] Evidently a reference to Ram's wife, Sita.

He only is a sadhu who searches wisely for the meaning of Shabd:
Only by searching can one obtain it; without effort it remains afar.
Both chaste and unchaste women are present in the world:
But the Good One is always present, under all conditions.
When the true light comes, other doors are closed;
Nothing else is visible, the Guru fulfils the highest hopes of all.

All remain in Uda Ji's protection; all abide with him:
Then the essence of life is known; then faith is established.
Uda Ji, you have through companionship, made me your servant;
You have made Amarpuri immortal; have opened the door of salvation;
The followers of Uda Das abide by his words.

A good woman is spotless: an unchaste woman is sinful.
At time of giving birth a woman is not pure; at such a time even a good woman is impure; she who lies with her husband is impure.
A good woman surpasses a bad woman, just as thirty-three gems surpass thirteen gems.
Birbhan and Raja Duryodhan had pure wives.

The True God

Where there is no righteousness, the people are poor;
In the court of God, the good and poor people are the same;
There is only one court of God (Allah); and there is one Master (Rabb);
See his appearance daily and remember him (sumran karna).
Remember only one and forget all others;
Let your attachment be always fixed on him; there is nothing external.
His name is everlasting, keep it constantly in your mind;
He has been called inaccessible (agam), and imperceptible (agochar);
Keep him in mind and you shall never be moved.
By holding to your convictions, you can reach your destination.

His appearance is true, but the way to Gurughat (God's place)
Is long, for it is surrounded by twenty-one circles (mandal);[1]
He who sees this inaccessible, imperceptible one becomes omniscient (avagat).
The True Guru has done me the favour of bestowing on me a fearless devotion;
Where there is no fear, all delusions are removed;
The True Guru has removed all my doubts and has given me Shabd fully.
He has looked on me with favor, he has given me the immortal herb.
He only is the real Sadhu who can recognize Shabd;
When one has made the first stage toward God, then light on Shabd begins to shine.
The lamp of knowledge has appeared to the servant Uda Ji (God)

[1] This is evidently some Hindu colouring.

O brave man, cherish Shabd in your heart; keep it in mind;
On the day of Uda Das' enlightenment, heaven and earth trembled;
O Brother, give up pride and violence (badh), then peace will be yours.
Let the True Guru appear; by remembering him there is great contentment.

Songs of Sadh Women

Though there is indifference on all sides, give gifts freely;
This is the mark of the True Guru, he is free from passion and anger;
He brings the joy of Shabd to the thirsty one.
Obey the teachings of Gorakh Ji, the permanent disciple of Uda Das.
Sham Devi sings that she has attained sight of the True Guru;
By seeing him she has become fearless and full of knowledge.

Song of Goma—Nirvana Bani

O Master of my soul, Servant of Uda, you the Omniscient (avagat),
Oh that you may come into the heart of this thy devotee (bhagat),
We hoped for one drop, but you fully quenched us with nectar;
Instead of talking about destroying the world, you have saved it;
Goma Bai praises thy name in word and song.

Often have I forgotten Goma Bai's admonition to sing his praise;
Sometimes instead of praise my mouth has uttered slighting words;
Rejecting Vedas, Koran, Puranas and Rabb, she calls Uda Das master of all.
For this I am truly thankful to Goma Bai;
O Sadhs, accept as your master him who was killed by the king's arrow.

Song of Raja Bai

Let Sadh companionship be sweet;
Onkar knows all things; this good teacher is our benefactor.
The world having become sinful is being carried away by a flood;
O Lord (Nath), they are full of delusion, because they have sinned greatly.
Ram and Krishna in their day ruled the devotees of the world;
With clasped hands Raja Bai sings, 'Save this world from destruction.'

Song of Gopi Chand

Salute your equals because all are servants;
O Brother! you will reap what you sow, no one will share the harvest.
He who lies awake planning how best to obey is dear to the True Guru;
O Master, thy Shabd has been milk to me, it has removed all darkness.
The Master appears; Gopi Chand, quite devoid of fear, is singing.

Song of Khan Ji

I have sacrificed all for the great name of Uda Das:
Having made supplication in his name, we drank to our full;
He is blessed who sings the praises of Ram and Krishna.
Gorakh Ji, pupil of Uda Das, has made us entirely fearless;
In presence of True Guru, Khan Ji falling at his feet, sings.

Song of Pand Ji[1]

To live one's life aimlessly is like ashes;
The Master has so written; his letters are the world's witness.
Yam[2] overcome, salvation obtained, my heart overflows;
He teaches us seeking for Shabd is necklace of good.

If you engage is honest trade, then take the profits fearlessly;
Mind is like a split pen; use both your eyes and your brain;
Exercise mentally, no thief can rob you of your mentality.
Wealth increases responsibility, but God carries us safely across;
Pand sings, 'Guru is blessed because he is mind and not body.'

O Sadh, the secret and source of salvation have been revealed;
Having obtained this boon, I awoke submerged in knowledge.
If you wish a good-natured discussion on religion, then seek Sadhs' fellowship.

Age accounts for a man's fatigue;
Shabd is the source of the Shastras,[3]
To attain the highest virtue, seek companionship of Sadhs;
Aroused by spear of devotion, your mind will be as sharp as a whip;
With the dagger of knowledge, you can chant Mantras as an arrow flies.
Meditating on the order of life, my mind is whipped into activity;
By singing and playing, one's mind is absorbed in the Good Guru.
He who serves the upper world can do you much good;
Pand says by obeying the Guru's will, wealth is obtained.
The speaker of truth is blessed because he has the mind of a devotee.

Jar Jodhan's Song

O Brother, behold his favoured people!
With tears, and open mind, Raja Harish Chandar has examined this thing;[4]

[1] Pand is probably a corruption of Pandit.
[2] The lord of death. [3] Hindu religious books.
[4] Harish Chandar was a character of Mahabharata. He gave his whole kingdom to charity, went to Benares, was reduced to very menial service, also his wife; through all their hardships they remained the devotees of truth. God being pleased, restored them to their former positions of power and pomp as he did Job.
He is also an historical character. See Keay's *A History of Hindi Literature*, pp. 91 ff.

O foolish man! why don't you learn to know him by praise?
Kabir, with hand and head asked for the gift of devotion (bhakti).
Gorakh Ji, disciple of Uda Das is the supporter of all truth;
Upon full revelation Jar Jodhan sings, 'God is One,' (i.e. Satavagat is).

Jar Jodhan's Song of Nirvana

Shabd has stood the test of my heart;
My pilgrimages in search of truth were all quite futile;
Having gradually secured the truth, the whole world is now mine.
This good instruction has come to me from Gorakh Ji;
In ecstatic mind, Jar Jodhan sings, 'Truth is the real support.'

Nirvana Song of Dan Ji, the Twentieth Sadh

O Sadhs! I, too, have received a revelation through the Shabd;
The world and night are under the control of the True Name.[1]
The order of Gorakh, pupil of Uda Das will surely be fulfilled;
Know him to be true, the All-giver, the Omnipresent.
The heart of the servant is in the hand of God (Satavagat)
From a water-drop the soul was made; from the five elements the body came forth.[2]
All material things are transitory;
Gorakh Ji has protected me from all fear.

About 'Naver'[3]

When any Sadh, man or woman, commits an offence the case is placed before the panchayat. The culprit is obliged to undergo *naver*. The council members call out in a loud voice 'Naver.' The guilty has to repeat the following in the presence of the panchayat:

Separating myself from Hindus and Muslims, I became a Sadh. Confessing my guilt, I hope that by depending more fully on the teachings of the Guru I shall become guiltless in the future.

By means of 'Naver' the sins of the Sadhs are cleansed. O Sadh Brothers, what shall I say of you who abuse the power (of God)? O Sadhs you have not the real power. Make an effort to find and appropriate this power.

[1] 'World' is 'Nine parts' namely (1) Ilavrati, (2) Ramyak, (3) Hiranyamay, (4) Kuru, (5) Hari, (6) Bharat (India), (7) Ketumal, (8) Bhadrashwa, (9) Kinpurush.—Names in the *Ramayana*.

[2] Ether, air, fire, water and earth.

[3] Probably from Hindi, 'Niwar,' to remove, defend.

Nirvana, Songs of Incarnation, by Birbhan Sadhs

O Master we are all thy children; thou bestowest gifts upon us;
There is no one equal to thee—thou the creator of all hearts;
Thou controlest the moon, sun, wind and water . . . thou art our Protector.
Among thy disciples are Ram, Lakhsman, Bharat and Shatrugan;
In every age men have praised thee; by thy order the world was made.
Gorakh Ji, disciple of Uda Das is my only Teacher;
In presence of the Good Guru, Birbhan sings, 'May the True Name always be in my mind.'

Second Song of Pand

The hermit (Yogi) living separate, practices asceticism;
He has spread the teachings of the Five Elements;
In his glad tidings, he emphasizes the value of the Three Virtues.[1]
Daily bear in mind the qualities of the Avagat (God);
O Soul! without realizing God (Brahm) fear cannot be eliminated;
Without understanding Shabd, the bonds of Karma cannot be loosed;
Jogi Das says all those who have learned the yogi and,
All who have given up passionate desires, have attained the good.

Birbhan's Incarnation

O Sadhs! by his greatness we see the True Guru, and true Devotion;
Renounce greed, enticements, pride; then eternal contentment will be your reward.
When you have put lust, anger and passion under control then,
Meekness, a forgiving spirit will control your heart.
Before the Teacher, Birbhan in song, obtains enjoyment of full salvation
The Sadhs call the incarnation of Birbhan, 'Nehkalank' (sinless).

Second Song of Birbhan

Our Master the True Guru has revealed to us his secrets;
Removing all doubt and illusion, we have found the truth;
A knowledge of Shabd fulfilled our desire by making us fearless.[2]
Gorakh Ji, disciple of Uda Das revealed the secret of life;
The same has formed a society of his servants;
Because of their greatness we remember Birbhan and the True Guru.

[1] *Sattva-gun*, goodness, virtue; *rajas-gun*, passion, foulness; *tamas-gun*, darkness, ignorance. (Sanskrit.)

[2] Philo says 'The soul once unyoked from the Logos will be cast away forever, without possibility of return.'

Birbhan the Sadh incarnation says that Uda Das our Master has revealed his secrets to us only, to no one else, not even to Ram, nor Krishna, nor to Muhammad. Birbhan is our true instructor.

Another Song of Birbhan

O Sadhs! all doubt is removed from my mind,
The True Teacher has commanded us to bow down to no one else;
This clear order we certainly understood from the very first.
When Shabd comes into our hearts, how can he remain unknown?
Physical fatigue, mental doubts are wholly removed instantly;
If you wish to be free from illusions, let Creator (Brahm) touch your body.
The True Guru appears, Birbhan sings, daily warning comes to us.

The meaning of the song is this: Uda Das has revealed his secrets to his disciples and warned them not to bow down to any one else. The Sadhs do not salam nor say 'Ram Ram' to any one belonging to another religion. They have made this their rule just as Birbhan has sung it; Sadhs call Uda Das their teacher, their creator and their Redeemer (Muktidata). They look upon Jogi Das and Birbhan as the incarnation of Ram and Lakhsman. When Aurengzeb was king in Delhi,[1] then Uda Das was their master and Birbhan was their incarnation, in Delhi.

Oh Sadhs, tell me, is the mention of this incarnation made in the Scriptures of any other religion, speak the truth, is it or is it not?[2]

Durga Das' Song of Ram's Invasion

From the East came the Hindus; from the West, the Muslims;
They tried to surround us, but we remained beyond their grasp.
The Sat Guru coming to us, explained the strategy of war.
Receiving words of encouragement from him, we put on our armour;
Having put on the armor of Shabd we became eager to fight.
The Sat Guru, being free from rebirths, appeared to Uda Das.[3]
He assured Uda Das that he was the True Name (Sat Nam).
O Sadhs, if you remember his name you will become fearless;
Durga Das sings, 'Let followers of Uda Das advance to the front.'
Sadhs appeared in battle in great splendour of weapons;
He who obeys orders and clears the field of enemies, is a brave man.

Evening Prayer of Peace

At every breath be present before God; through the eight watches of the day act upon his will. Bow down to Uda Das and the good company of Sadhs.

[1] 1659–1707. [2] The answer implied is: 'No, of course not.' The prose notes are Prithi Lal's.

[3] The expression is 'Eighty-four lakhs of births.'

Third Song of Pand

In the First Age man is as prone to do evil as the sun to shine;
Similarly but more so, the Second Age brings man to shamelessness;
Advancing to the Third, man's dual nature becomes depraved;
If man misses his chance of salvation in the fourth Age, he is hopeless.
This earth, full of delusions, brings many men into wrong paths;
Missing this opportunity, when can you hope for another?
The greater the number of rebirths, the more opportunity for salvation.

Clever men of other religions appear to us like locusts,
That is, in comparison to Uda Das' disciples they are unsophisticated.
While the eye-sight is keen and strong, no one can attack;
Even though my body become frail, my mind will entertain no doubts;
Though my body fall to pieces, even then my mind shall remain optimistic;
Now we enjoy earthly affluence; some day this body will return to ashes.

Pand says he has never seen such a servant (as described above);
He is so obscure that only a few can apprehend him;
Even by prayerful worship, only a remnant learn to know him (God).
Father, mother, and children are all mortal;
O Man! look on the world but remember that its beauty lasts but four days;
Having obtained a wealth of gold, can you, will you forget the Priceless Jewel?
All life is but a dream; hence do not be proud;
When the final day comes, O Brother, rejoice in that day;
Except the one whom you worship, no one will go with you;
Without the object of worship, O man you are as one dead.

Awake, O foolish man, life is fast slipping away;
O foolish one! never again will such a day be yours.
You have ignored the diamond and cherished a (kauri) shell;
Passing by the pure water, you have drunk from the ditch;
A stigma on your heart has contaminated your love (prem);
O soul! will you inhabit this same body, time after time?

What a mistake to try to find the holy river without effort;
Is this your policy to obtain morality without great effort?
People who are instinctively good, have conquered evil.

The joys of evil are like an ornament whose lustre soon fades;
Evil says, Enjoy these worldly things while you may;
Thinking it a small thing, men do not realize its baneful influence.

O Sadhs, in all ages, matter and spirit are at variance (enemies);
The world is nothing but an ocean of delusions;
The visible earth is an hallucination.

If you neglect your worship, you will quickly go astray,
To remember God, this is the first and last commandment.

In the market you have made a purchase which puts you in debt;
Not only is it a cheap commodity, but it means the loss of your original capital;
Now, bankrupt, you must face the True Teacher.

The true servant has crossed the stream of life, conquering all enemies;
O servant, what a great pleasure and reward is now yours;
Pand says, 'Live such a life as described above.'

THE END

BIBLIOGRAPHY

HISTORIES AND GAZETTEERS

Government Census Reports
The Farrukhabad Gazetteer (U.P.)
Rohtak Gazetteer (Punjab) Vol. III, 1910
Karnal Gazetteer (Punjab) 1890
The Imperial Gazetteer Vol. XII, 1908
Fatehgarh Court Records
J. N. SARKAR, *History of Aurengzib*, Vol. III
WM. IRVINE, I.C.S., *History of Farrukhabad, 1713–1897* (Urdu)
VINCENT SMITH, *Akbar the Great Mogul*
VINCENT SMITH, *Oxford History of India*

ARTICLES ON THE SADHS

H. H. WILSON, *The Religious Sects of the Hindus*, Vol. I
Encyclopædia of Religion and Ethics, Vol. IX
SIR WM. CROOKE, *Tribes and Castes of the North-west Provinces*
C.M.S. Register of 1819 'Authentic Accounts of the Saadhs,' articles by HENRY FISHER
Transactions of the Royal Asiatic Society, Vol. I, article by WILLIAM TRANT

HINDI WRITINGS

Prabha Magazine, March, 1920
UMRAU SINGH SADH, *Sadh Susamachar*
Writings of UMRAU SINGH SADH and other Sadhs
Nirvana Gyan, the Sadh Scriptures

MISCELLANEOUS

J. N. FARQUHAR, *The Crown of Hinduism*
TRUMPP, *The Sikh Granth*
Bernier's Travels
N. MACNICOL, *Indian Theism*
DUBOIS, *Hindu Manners, Customs, etc.*
Sir WM. CROOKE, *Popular Religion and Folklore of Northern India*
BHANDARKAR, *Encyclopædia of Indo-Aryan Research*
JOHN NEWTON, *The American Presbyterian Mission in India*
SIR EDWARD MACLAGAN, *The Jesuits of the Great Mogul*, 1932
J. N. FARQUHAR, *The Armed Ascetics of India* (Unpublished)
WM. IRVINE, *Journal of the Asiatic Society of Bengal*, Vol. XLVII
C. J. BROWN, *The Coins of India*

INDEX